Tsunami Watch

Power, Pain and Progress in the American Narrative

Barry Howard and Daniel Kosten

ISBN 978-1-64003-450-1 (Paperback)
ISBN 978-1-64003-451-8 (Hardcover)
ISBN 978-1-64003-452-5 (Digital)

Covenant Books, Inc.
11661 Hwy 707
Murrells Inlet, SC 29576
www.covenantbooks.com

This book is dedicated to

*Holly & Amie and
Noah, Hannah, Hillary, Nadine,
Rebekah, Abraham, and Joshua*

CONTENTS

PROLOGUE

As with any work in which vocation and life mission are aligned with authorship, this effort is a labor forged and refined over many years. Having worked in the relief and development sector throughout their careers, the authors balance experience, empathy, and pragmatism while engaging some of the most difficult issues facing numerous contemporary societies. It is with a passion to see these issues resolved in a healthy and sustainable manner that this publication was approached. The journey of learning is a perpetual one and rife with the pain of failure and the joy of epiphany. So it is and continues to be with the authors.

Conventional wisdom would logically dictate that the societal conundrums unearthed within these pages should have resolved themselves over time, without becoming increasingly severe. Unfortunately, the entropy of bigotry and isolationism is not a natural process, but rather one that comes only through self-actualization on a macro-level and by consciously grinding the mill to a halt. While this does, perhaps, speak to the base nature of humanity when left unchecked, hope springs eternal that inspiration may spark a change in individual beliefs and actions, which might then spark a greater movement.

Our collective tendencies drive us to live myopically within the constraints of what we have been told, what we have seen around us, and how we have interpreted the sliver of the world in which we exist. Herein lies the opportunity to take a peek inside our hearts and minds to what lies beneath the thick veneer of our limited worldviews and faulty paradigms. An introspective self-analysis is but one intended outcome of the work, while tangible, sustainable change in society is the endgame.

James Baldwin—an American novelist, playwright, and social critic—stated, "The great force of history comes from the fact that we carry it within us, are unconsciously controlled by it . . . History is literally present in all that we do." Baldwin's statement captures the hope which inspired this work. We are not doomed to repeat our past mistakes or perpetuate current ones. Rather, we have the rich tapestry of our predecessors: personages, sovereign entities, and, most importantly, affinity groups through the ages who have struggled with the exact same problems we struggle with today.

Some of this material will be perceived and processed in third person by the reader. So it may be, and that is fine and good. A more personable and intimate style may have been in order at times, but continuity demands a motif. That said, it should also be noted that the authors who composed this work have no political axe to grind. The subject matter of this work transcends ideological sects. Our end game is that it will speak to each reader, individually.

The reader should be forewarned at the outset of this journey that honest introspection and transparent evaluation of each facet within these pages will produce the greatest outcome for each one of us. There is no singular villain identified here. There is, rather, only the human condition to which we are all indentured servants until our brief time on this planet comes to a close. The authors recognize that their success rests fully upon whether the concepts, admonitions, and recommendations laid out are the catalyst for lasting change in both the heart (what we truly believe) and the hand (what we actually do when no one is looking).

May what you read be compelling enough to penetrate your heart, poignant enough to catalyze your mind and tongue with truth, and powerful enough to drive your hand to necessary action.

Chapter 1

Tsunami of Angst

Long, long ago, a great empire's seat of power rested in the city of Rome. And while its geographic boundaries were exceeded by British, Mongolian, and well over twenty other empires throughout history, one of its unique qualities separated it from its peers. The Romans' ability to effectively govern and spread Hellenistic culture and Greek thought throughout the known Western world remains a marvel. Subjugation was accomplished by a policy of integration without cultural disruption. In effect, the Romans "absorbed" their vanquished foes and allowed them to continue to do business as usual.

America, not unlike the Romans, purports a policy of inclusiveness, unrivalled in the modern world. Forged of European immigrants, Native Americans, African Americans, Asian Americans, and South and Central American immigrants, the "Great American Salad Bowl," like the Roman Empire, is supposedly a diverse cultural forum aligned under one nation—a true republic.

But is it?

There is a deep unrest in the land, indicative of a gathering storm. A tempest of angst and simmering anger catalyzed by no clear cause. Partisan polarization has never been more extreme. Public demonstrations and protest are becoming increasingly volatile. Ideological fervor has driven zealots on all fronts into a veritable frenzy.

Why?

This work is an effort to identify, analyze, and summarize the tsunami of unrest washing over our country. Tsunamis are ocean waves generated by earthquakes or underwater landslides. A Japanese word meaning "harbor wave," a tsunami is not a single wave but rather a series of waves. Reaching speeds of up to six hundred miles an hour, they exceed even the velocity of modern commercial airlines. The waves are not singular but rather a series of events that can be traced back to one singular cause. They deliver unfathomable devastation, impacting areas normally considered safe havens like harbors. Tsunamis move quickly and are often difficult to detect with the naked eye, creating a sense of powerlessness and a loss of control.

America rests on the precipice of several key decisions that will define our nation well beyond the next century. (We will use America throughout this work to refer more specifically to the United States of America, and note the same in advance for those who share the continent of North America with us.) Fifty years after the race riots and peace marches of the sixties, we elected an African American President but yet seem to be no closer to ethnic symbiosis at a societal level.

We ponder options to keep at bay an influx of immigration while Lady Liberty holds a tablet in her hands, citing the immortal words of Emma Lazarus:

Give me your tired, your poor,

Your huddled masses yearning to breathe free,

The wretched refuse of your teeming shore.

Send these, the homeless, tempest-tossed, to me:

I lift my lamp beside the golden door.

Interestingly, the verses did not reach such significance overnight. The sonnet inscription was primarily unacknowledged until after Lazarus's death, when a New York arts patron found it in a small portfolio of poems written in 1883 to raise money for the construction of the statue's pedestal. Immediately, Georgina Schuyler was moved by the lines and endeavored to have its last five stanzas become a permanent part of the statue itself. Two decades later, schoolbooks began to include the sonnet and Irving Berlin wrote it into a Broadway musical.

In "The New Colossus," Lazarus compares the symbol of the United States with what many consider the perfect symbol of the Greek and Roman era: the Colossus of Rhodes. Her comparison proved appropriate, for Bartholdi created the Statue of Liberty with the well-known Colossus in mind. What Bartholdi did not intend, however, was for the Statue of Liberty to become a symbol of welcome for thousands of European immigrants. Lazarus's poem forever made the Statue of Liberty a beacon of welcome for immigrants *leaving* their native countries.

Why then has there been such a significant shift in the corporate American mindset in regard to the influx of immigrants? While most Americans would not hesitate to agree for the allowance of more skilled and educated newcomers (a "brain drain" on other nations), those with lesser credentials have begun to drive animosity and resentment.

Some of this is, logically, attributed to the labor pool disruption in American society and alleged increased competition for lower-paying jobs. But in a global economy growing tighter each day, the necessity of finding alternate ways to compete in the world's economic landscape is a stark reality and an obvious road ahead. Unless America can find viable ways to bring manufacturing back into its geographical boundaries, the historical labor pool in American society will be redirected by Adam Smith's *Invisible Hand* toward reasonable alternatives to derive a financial return, vocationally.

No, the problem lies deeper than one related directly to economic impetus. It is born of a rift growing between cultures. A "clash of civilizations," to coin Samuel Huntington's immortal nomenclature. Further, it is the result of unhealed "wounds" within our society, and the conscious and subconscious reaction and fears of the classical majority, juxtaposed with an unwillingness to seek reconciliation at the most fundamental levels.

Ironically, the greatest chasm in the equity of human justice transcends the specific nature of this work. That is, the inequality of genders throughout history. Addressed herein are American-centric societal conundrums, although they may be relevant in other national contexts. Gender disparity and injustice is a global phenomenon, which has been a theme in human civilization since its inception. This epic travesty deserves its own thesis and is simply not the intrinsic subject matter of the work at hand.

This work's commitment to pragmatism and unmitigated truth will be a bitter pill for some to swallow, especially those entrenched in specific ideologies. For some, though, for those who have ears to hear, malleable hearts, and the willingness to renew their minds, it will provide a refreshing set of epiphanies.

> *Don't bend; don't water it down; don't*
> *try to make it logical; don't edit*
> *your own soul according to the fashion. Rather,*
> *follow your most intense obsessions mercilessly.*
>
> *—Franz Kafka*

CHAPTER 2

Strange Days
The Trump Factor

As this chapter was being written, Donald Trump was the Republican nominee for the 2016 general election. His personality and biography are certainly a thing of lore, and . . . love him or hate him . . . he is a media magnet and a cultural icon.

There is no effort here to make a qualitative analysis of the merits of Donald Trump as a person, a leader, or even a beacon of general interest. Rather, of relevance now and in the future is the ability to understand what about Trump's fundamental nature, and his proposed political and social positions, poised him to capture the support of tens of millions of American citizens. Trump could, conceivably, be the best or worst leader in history. Only history can make that call, and so this commentary is not interested in praising him nor bashing him.

That said, extrapolating quotations from Donald Trump to support any thesis is akin to picking ingredients from an infinitely stocked cupboard. There is no shortage of varying perspectives and profound statements; some of which adjust over time. Again, we are not visiting the accuracy or inaccuracy of these Trumpian virtues or vices but rather what elements about him have catalyzed his current status.

Through it all, there are archetypical themes we can derive from Trump's popularity, which transcend the basic, rational arguments, such as his ability to manage the nation's fiscal issues or the utility he brings to Washington as an outsider. Trump extols his personal strength and power. He, in fact, exudes a great deal of strength and power. Additionally, he promises national strength and power.

So how does he propose to infuse this into the American paradigm?

Primarily, Donald Trump's position is one which presupposes a Copernican theory for America's role in the world. Ignoring the fundamental nature of cultural globalization and the dynamic flow of immigration over the centuries as the cornerstone for the American model, Trump purports an alternative to build strength and power in the nation. By locking down the gates of the country, he proposes to stem the tide of drugs and other evils that flow into the nation, along with illegal immigrants.

This position is one that has gathered quite a bit of strength with the American public on many levels. It is, of note, a policy that would theoretically lock down the power shift tsunamis, which this book addresses. Keep the current population in stasis, and keep the majority as the majority.

Additionally, such a position addresses an ambiguous fear that many Americans feel but cannot name, which is rooted in economic turmoil. At some level, many of us sense the presence of growing economies outside our gates, which, for the first time since the 1950s, could usurp America's role as the premier superpower. That is, understandably, a somewhat scary concept for those on the receiving end of declination. Nevertheless, an isolationist reaction to this concern is truly the last thing that will curb it.

There is also a more primal appeal in Trump's ability to project the power and strength already addressed. Weary, are many Americans, of the knowledge that other world leaders dictate foreign policy to the United States. Donald Trump promises to take that power back. And while he guarantees negotiation to be the paramount activity in his purview, he couples that promise with the assurance that America will no longer be on the losing end of any deal.

What does all of this mean?

Donald Trump is but one man and is really only an extended expression of the corporate will and concern of a significant sector of the American populace. The world is pressing into and changing the power structure for one of the wealthiest segments of the global population. To react to such a shift is only natural . . . but how we react is pivotal.

That Donald Trump won the 2016 general election is not consequential to this publication, so much as the fact that he was ever a candidate in the first place. Whether buoyed on the tide of extremist sentiment during the primary elections or chosen to serve by a larger portion of the general electorate, Trump's very presence in the discussion, the very fact that this much of the story is already in the books to tell, is indicative of the tense sentiment here identified.

While the reasons for Trump's popularity may vary from person to person, one common theme transcends the variations and weaves a telling narrative about our collective concerns regarding globalization and our role in a shrinking world.

CHAPTER 3

Gerrymandered Folly

Nationalism is an infantile disease. The measles of mankind.

—Albert Einstein

The nation-state is a long-standing concept, existing long before the great pyramids were constructed, as mankind moved away from small agrarian groups to more complex communities. Such a transition provided mutual utility for groupings through increased diversity of skills, services, and production. Small towns became larger towns, which in turn became cities. Those first cities were surrounded by small settlements and towns and comprised an epicenter for the city-state concept. Inevitably, regional parity led to coalitions between the city-states, which evolved into the first nation-states—consolidated seats of power for large homogeneous populations.

There is significant merit in this social evolution, as it benefits all individuals through mutual utility. Wealth is increased exponentially. Personal and corporate safety are ensured through urbanization and military development.

The list goes on. But with every set of virtues comes an off-setting string of vices. When esoteric groups, regardless of how small or large, begin to cement their ethos and define themselves as an independent entity, mutually exclusive from other groups, values begin to formulate that often lead to detrimental relationships with outsiders and opposing worldviews.

Of note, it is important to realize that this treatise recognizes the intrinsic beauty of culture and the marvelous diversity between self-actualized groups of humanity. It is a palette of colors weaving a tapestry of humanity that defies the advent of an Orwellian future of automatons. Nevertheless, the fundamental value of culture itself should be recognized simply as a set of behaviors and beliefs that are common to any given group. Whether on a macro-level, anyone's national culture is simply the natural manifestation and evolution of how their particular group decided to eat, dance, sing, speak, think, and interact. It is sometimes a product of necessity driven by external forces and other times the result of a few forceful opinions early in the life cycle of a culture that defined its trajectory for centuries to come.

As culture develops, the parity of the individuals inside its circle draws lines, both literally and figuratively, to protect all they deem fundamentally better than its alternatives and more often than not to perpetuate, advance, and even impose their ethos on dissimilar groups. Herein lies the fundamental problem with any culture. The group begins to believe it has the most viable, if not only viable, model for living and thinking, and thus seeks to protect and often replicate itself at great cost.

This is not necessarily a bad thing. We all pitch our tents around the camp of that with which we are most familiar. The nature of humanity is to improve its current situation, and certainly creating a haven of comfort based on familiarity is conducive to that very primal tendency. But when any group begins to perceive its culture or fundamental nature as "better" than that of others, many things happen, which we do not need to fully unpack here. War itself is a derivative of this phenomenon, as are many of mankind's most dire ills.

Nationalism, and subsequently fascism when unchecked, is the inevitable result of this paradigm, left to its logical outcome. The development of the nation-state creates a bubble of myopic beliefs, driving both the nation-state itself, and those within it, toward a collectively introspective view of all varying contexts. Thus, it is but a mirage—a protective reflex forged of corporate self-preservation and a lack of knowledge and understanding about how other people might live, think, and feel. Nevertheless, it has been the functional model for geographical and cultural gathering and identification since the earliest days of human civilization and certainly it will not change in the foreseeable future.

So why bother analyzing something entrenched so deeply in the human societal experience? If it is our inevitable pattern to find and cling to that which we know best, what is the counter-narrative to an alternate solution?

As stated, the tendency for human beings to identify and gather together with similar human beings is a mainstay for the species. In fact, the virtues outweigh the vices, all things considered. But the detriment of nationalism is something that should simply be a point of awareness for the enlightened individual within any society. This would best be described as awareness of our unwavering capacity to believe that our way is the better way, the best way . . . and even the only way. Understanding that truth is the pathway to counteracting our perceptions toward our neighbors—across the street and across the ocean.

The quote opening this chapter has catalyzed a great deal of speculation, but Einstein meant exactly what he said. Taken from a book written by the man himself, *The World As I See It,* was published in 1934. It was clear that Einstein saw firsthand how nationalism impedes the confrontation and resolution of real challenges facing humanity at any given point in history, and it must be deprioritized as childish.

What can we say, then, about nationalism in the American context and how it has shaped the dynamics being examined in this work? Put simply, few nation-states have had a more myopic view of their singular greatness than the USA in the history of mankind. Only a few civilizations in history, at the height of their power, have experienced the temptation toward national pride the way Americans do. America's immense wealth and power and its singular place as the world's greatest force in the modern age gives its citizens a unique view from a previously undiscovered mountaintop. Within that nationalistic phenomenon exists an internal reality, relevant primarily to the ruling class or historical majority of the nation.

That reality is the fundamental belief that the prevailing majority's ideology is the primary catalyst for all of America's success, and thus the wellspring of its greatness.

It is only natural that the majority would perceive that its own belief system and values dictated the success or failure of its respective nation-state. This is not an illogical perspective, as it certainly holds water and is to some degree true.

The dilemma lies in the fact that the majority or ruling class, particularly in America, is unique and specific to its singular point in time. America is a set of rolling waves of immigrants. Certainly 400 hundred years ago the ethos of the nation could be attributed primarily to a static monolithic engine, but much has changed. The America of today is a collective result of many cultures woven into a fundamentally European functional construct. The infrastructure for the Great Experiment remains intact, but the players involved in the experiment do not.

Why then do we insist on embracing a narrative that purports the paramount utility of one segment of the population? In fact, it is one of the oldest of human habits that drives this forward . . . our desire to identify, condone, embrace, and replicate the things that validate us personally. Thus, the diminishing majority, is perpetually faced with the stark reality of a slowly-changing ethnic landscape, while struggling to align past, present, and future greatness with its own worldview and value system. Put simply, within the gerrymandered borders of our own nation, we have become a group of increasingly distinct nation-states.

CHAPTER 4

America the Beautiful, the Great, the Mortal

I met a traveller from an antique land
Who said: "Two vast and trunkless legs of stone
Stand in the desert . . . Near them, on the sand,
Half sunk, a shattered visage lies, whose frown,
And wrinkled lip, and sneer of cold command,
Tell that its sculptor well those passions read
Which yet survive, stamped on these lifeless things,
The hand that mocked them, and the heart that fed:
And on the pedestal these words appear:
"My name is Ozymandias, king of kings:
Look on my works, ye Mighty, and despair!"
Nothing beside remains. Round the decay
Of that colossal wreck, boundless and bare
The lone and level sands stretch far away.

—*Percy Bysshe Shelley*

There is a saying in modern culture that states, "There are only two things certain in life: death and taxes." While it is a humorous commentary on the consistency of taxation in any culture, the adage is only half true. What is certain is death. And though that sounds like a bleak forecast, it is simply the inevitable journey that all living things traverse. Obedient to the second law of thermodynamics (total entropy of an isolated system always increases over time), death is a phenomenon that humanity and all of nature reckon with, to no avail. While you can dodge him for a season, the Reaper is coming.

Similarly, macro-entities also have finite life cycles. This is evidenced throughout history. Egypt and China both had remarkably long runs, but even their dynasties waned and transformed into completely new creations. Rome is celebrated as the beacon of Hellenistic stability, but in truth its era of epic greatness lasted only a few hundred years. Doubtlessly, during the reign of Augustus Caesar, no able-minded Romans could have conceived of their empire ever coming to an end.

The modern era is less a respecter of nations than the ancient past. They rise and fall in natural cycles. Not long ago the greatest power at sea, and arguably on land, England has since been relegated to a spot on the top-ten list of superpowers and has never reclaimed the glory of its greatness since post–World War II. This is not necessarily a negative thing. It is a natural thing. It is a healthy evolution and a phenomenon that is empirically proven over millennia. To think that any country, including the United States of America, should be exempt from the same is a blind fallacy.

To the point, in *The Fate of Empires and Search for Survival,* Sir John Glubb states, "Empires do not normally begin or end on a certain date. There is normally a gradual period of expansion and then a period of decline. The resemblance in the duration of these great powers may be queried. Human affairs are subject to many chances, and it is not to be expected that could be calculated with mathe-matical accuracy."[1] Glubb notes the following dates for several well-recognized empires:

Assyria:	859-612 B.C.E.
Persia:	538-330 B.C.E.
Greece:	331-100 B.C.E.
Rome (Rep):	260-27 B.C.E.
Rome (Emp):	27 B.C.E. – 190 C.E.
Arabian:	634-880 C.E.
Mameluke:	1250-1517 C.E.
Ottoman:	1320-1570 C.E.
Spain:	1500-1750 C.E.
Romanov:	1682-1916 C.E.
British:	1700-1944 C.E.

[1] Glubb J. (1976), The Fate of Empires and Search for Survival, William Blackwood & Sons, Edinburgh

In the same spirit, let it be stated from the outset that the authors of this work are not purporting the end of America or acting as harbingers of its eventual decline and fall. We, as Americans ourselves, would be the first to express that the model that America has created, the Capitalist Republic with remarkable allowance for personal freedoms and private ownership, is, hands down, the best model with the highest utility, thus far realized in history. That may be a strong and an arguably subjective statement, but it is not unfounded. It is based upon the ability of America to balance itself politically and economically in such a way that an abnormally large percentage of citizens receive an abnormally high level of utility. It is the rare and epic phenomenon of a prosperous middle class. What does that mean?

The US was created in such a way that private citizens, excepting slaves, were given the tools and the allowances to affect their own destinies. In many, if not most, nations, billions of individuals are born and cemented into their social and economic context. In yet other nations where there is a bit more play in class movement, there is still a very tight constraint on mobility which is generally governed by an elite ruling class or, at the very least, an elite economic class. But the United States of America is different. Interestingly, an important reason for that difference is as much a national "worldview" as it is the structure of the country's laws, policies, and freedoms.

In America, most (not all, but most) citizens have an intrinsic understanding that they could become wealthy or powerful or famous by working hard enough, or by some other approach to realize an improved situation. Regardless of whether they do or do not have the ability to pull it off and whether or not they ever actually do improve their station in life, somewhere deep inside almost all Americans there is an understanding that they live in a place where that is possible. That is not the case in other nations. Furthermore, most Americans who have not visited nor delved first-hand into other cultures have no concept of how a severely fatalistic worldview can affect a collective group of individuals who adhere to that view. Americans, on the contrary, believe things can get better, and so assume they will get better.

This is, in effect, the American Dream—the belief that any citizen is equipped with the freedoms and rights to craft his or her own destiny, both economically and socially. In that context, America is unique in history. Never before has any other nation created a cohesive belief system that embraces this worldview so universally. This is why the Bill Gates and Steve Jobs and, in the past, the Henry Fords, Cornelius Vanderbilts, J. D. Rockefellers and J. P. Morgans all created something big from something small from which thousands of others benefited. We have nurtured an environment of confidence and innovation that is mutually beneficial.

Do not think for a moment that there are not just as many Gates, Jobs, and Rockefellers in Africa, proportionally, than there are here. The same potential exists in any group of human beings around the globe. It is their environment and their worldview that constrains them. They are simply entrenched in systems that require them to live beneath a very low ceiling of economic allowance and personal freedoms and are also programmed from their earliest years to embrace a (generally fatalistic) worldview that is counteractive to everything most young Americans come to understand and believe about latent human potential and "what might be."

But things are changing. A smaller, tighter global community fueled by social media, real-time communication, and interaction cross-culturally has awakened many sleeping giants throughout the world. These giants are not metaphors for nations or economic entities as much as they are actual sectors of humanity (national borders aside) who have come to understand that the American Dream is possible for them as well even within their own nation. For some groups and locations, this is a steeper uphill climb than for others, where governmental and economic structures are adjusting to make allowance for this colossal level of self-discovery in which individuals worldwide are engaging.

What does this mean for us as Americans? Well, it really does not mean anything fundamentally "bad" or "terrible," apart from the fact that we have competition from a world that is awakening from a long slumber of oppression. China, India, Korea, and many other countries are figuring things out, and the Gates, Jobs, and Rockefellers in their midst are no longer fettered. It is a new day, and there are other players on the field.

For a country that for the past seventy or so years has understood itself to be the undisputed world power both militarily and economically, this may come as a hard pill to swallow. But it is, in reality, a good thing. You see, there are two ways of looking at any market. One is to view the marketplace as a finite pie that is sliced into varying-sized pieces for respective pie lovers to savor . . . a lot or a little. Such a model is founded on a belief that a market is naturally constrained and that a smaller piece of the pie means the sky is falling.

There is another way to view this same model that, although quite simple, is an epiphany for many. In this model, the pie itself is the variable, not the amount or size of the slices. A smaller piece of a pie that is one hundred times larger than its tiny counterpart is a whole lot better than carving out an additional 10 percent of the skimpy finite pie. And so it is with the changing world in which we live. While America worries itself about the size of its slice, the rest of the world is cooking up a much larger pie. As the saying goes, "Keep your eye on the doughnut, not the hole."

This economic model is but one facet of a wider transition going on globally. Without question, America still rules the roost with regard to personal freedoms and a myriad of other evaluative considerations. America is great and beautiful, but it is also a nation in a state of change, just like every nation before it. It could theoretically become even more powerful, eclipsing anything previously observed, or it could recede. Neither is good, and neither is bad. What is relevant is how much utility that wide swathe of citizens within the borders of the nation enjoy. That is the endgame, and that is the measure by which America will test its mettle.

CHAPTER 5

Of the People, by the People, for the People . . .

*Republics are created by the virtue, public spirit, and
intelligence of the citizens. They fall, when the wise are
banished from the public councils, because they dare
to be honest, and the profligate are rewarded, because
they flatter the people, in order to betray them.*

—*Joseph Story*

Vital to understanding the nature of America and fathoming its historical struggles and current challenges is understanding how it is structured. Many Americans do not understand, and so here we provide a very succinct overview of how the collective will of hundreds of millions of people within America's sovereign borders is accommodated.

As a predominately two-party country, Americans often fail to understand the very distinct differences between a democracy and a republic. It can be reasonably argued that the current two-party system (Democrats and Republicans) only lends itself to exasperating this confusion.

This lack of clarity is driven by numerous catalysts. Foreign policy objectives have often been summarized as an attempt to export democracy around the world. The success of such an exercise has been at best mixed, but it further confuses who America is as a nation. Most US citizens would convey that they are part of a democracy, not a republic. This is not the case.

Before skipping this chapter on dry political structure as an unnecessary study in tedium, take a moment to become familiar with this distinction, as it is intricately intertwined and critical to the overall premise of this work.

A true democracy is a political system in which the majority have ultimate control and the minority are subject to the will of the majority. It has been described historically as mob rule and, while on a small scale is the purest reflection of a group's corporate will, it quickly engages the law of diminishing returns for larger populations. Classically, within true democracies, it becomes acceptable over time to utilize minority populations as scapegoats for the eventual demise of the democracy.

True democracies generally last a little less than two hundred years. Greece in the fifth century serves as the paragon example, and historically there are very few true democracies. Examined closely, it becomes apparent that the life cycle of a democracy, often born of a corporate desire to break free from any species of bondage, follows a predictable pattern. That pattern often follows a cycle: (1) bondage, (2) liberties, (3) prosperity, (4) individualism, (5) selfishness, (6) dependencies, and finally back into bondage. It is the model expressed in George Orwell's *Animal Farm* and one that history has proven time and again.

During the conception and development of the United States of America, our founding fathers knew that true democracy would be dangerous and something to be avoided at all cost. John Adams stated, "Remember, democracy never lasts long. It soon wastes, exhausts, and murders itself. There was never a democracy yet that did not commit suicide."

True democracies are most strongly advocated for in the midst of severe national decline—while the nation-state is in its death throes, and quality of life is lowest for its constituency. The cycle demonstrates that, at their birth, the loud call is for one and all; however, during their decline, the call is for leadership from a select group of individuals or a single powerful leader. That call can often be disguised as being in the best interests and protection of everyone while, in effect, it is an attempt to central-ize power. This is evidenced historically, perhaps most poignantly, in the speedy transition from the terrors of the French Revolution to an emperor named Napoleon. When there is no longer a majority, what happens in a democracy? It ceases.

A republic is based on rule by law. Those laws are writ-ten and approved by individuals elected by the population to represent them. They include constitutions, declara-tions, bills, and charters that establish certain inalienable rights. Those rights are for all the people and not solely for the benefit of the majority. Such laws place a check on how the majority population interacts with the minority population. In such a system, not only does *lex* supersede *rex*, but it is paramount to *turba* as well (Latin for *law, king,* and *mob* respectively).

The founding fathers intentionally chose to establish the United States of America as a republic. Well aware of the self-destructive nature of true democracies, they hoped to establish a system of governance that would far exceed and outlive any democracy. Alexander Hamilton stated that "We are now forming a republican government. Real liberty is neither found in despotism or the extremes of democracy, but in moderate government." Those wise men codified a republican form of government that would outlast all democracies before it. In the US Constitution, Article IV Section 4 states that "The United States shall guarantee to every State in this Union a Republican Form of Government . . ."

In light of rapidly changing demographics within our nation, it is quite possible that we may see a call for a move toward a true democracy so as to redefine the current constraints of the law by the majority. That call will most likely be exercised subtly. If it does occur publicly, it will be accomplished through the argument that it is occurring for the protection of all the people and for the well-being of the country. Law and order are exalted as long as it strengthens and affirms whatever position we hold. In such cases, it can otherwise be perceived as an obstruction to be mitigated.

There exists already a redefining of the American system of law and order. This has become particularly evident in the position the nation takes toward exercising individual judgment on the actions of others. Our system of law has established that one is innocent until proven guilty; yet common practice, particularly within the context of the American media, is for unqualified entities and market-driven fervor to serve as a court of public opinion.

The takeaway here is an understanding that true democracy does not work. And while it may appear to be a purer, more logical reflection of the will of the people, it fails as much ideologically as it does logistically. The republic we live in is part of that Great Experiment and one of the cornerstones of America's stability.

CHAPTER 6

Pearls of Great Price

A man went to Guru Nanak Sahib and asked, "What's the value of life?"

Guru Nanak ji gave him one stone and said, "Find out the value of this stone, but don't sell it."

The man took the stone to an Orange Seller and asked him what its cost would be. The Orange Seller saw the shiny stone and said, "You can take 12 oranges and give me the stone." The man apologized and said that the guru has asked him not to sell it.

He went ahead and found a vegetable seller. "What could be the value of this stone?" He asked the vegetable seller. The seller saw the shiny stone and said, "Take one sack of potatoes and give me the stone." The man again apologized and said he can't sell it.

Further ahead, he went into a jewelry shop and asked the value of the stone. The jeweler saw the stone under a lens and said, "I'll give you 50 Lakhs for this stone." When the man shook his head, the jeweler said, "Alright, alright, take 2 crores, but give me the stone." The man explained that he can't sell the stone.

Further ahead, the man saw a precious stone's shop and asked the seller the value of this stone. When the precious stone's seller saw the big ruby, he lay down a red cloth and put the ruby on it. Then he walked in circles around the ruby and bent down and touched his head in front of the ruby. "From where did you bring this priceless ruby from?" he asked.

"Even if I sell the whole world and my life, I won't be able to purchase this priceless stone."

Stunned and confused, the man returned to the guru and told him what had happened. "Now tell me what is the value of life, guru ji?"

Guru Nanak said, "The answers you got from the Orange Seller, the Vegetable Seller, the Jeweler and the Precious Stone's Seller explain the value of our life . . . You may be a precious stone, even priceless, but people will value you based on their financial status, their level of information, their belief in you, their motive behind entertaining you, their ambition, and their risk taking ability. But don't fear, you will surely find someone who will discern your true value."

—Guru Nanak

The stability and sustainability of any culture is best measured by the value it places on people. That value can neither solely be fathomed by its rhetoric nor its founding documents, but must be evaluated each day by its practices and by the condition of its populace.

In 1776, a committee was formed by Congress to draft a document to be used to set forth the case to the world why the Colonies were declaring independence. The Committee of Five consisted of John Adams, Roger Sherman, Benjamin Franklin, Robert R. Livingston, and Thomas Jefferson. Jefferson drafted the original document; Adams and Franklin made some changes. It was introduced to Congress on July 1, 1776 and three days later, on July 4, with some edits and deletions, the church bells of Philadelphia rang out that the Declaration had been adopted unanimously by the thirteen colonies represented in the Congress.

The second paragraph of the Declaration states,

> *We hold these truths to be self-evident, that all men are created equal, that they are endowed by their Creator with certain unalienable Rights, that among these are Life, Liberty and the pursuit of Happiness.—That to secure these rights, Governments are instituted among Men, deriving their just powers from the consent of the governed,—That whenever any Form of Government becomes destructive of these ends, it is the Right of the People to alter or to abolish it, and to institute new Government, laying its foundation on such principles and organizing its powers in such form, as to them shall seem most likely to effect their Safety and Happiness.*

In that statement, the value of human life is established along with a number of related and priceless principles. The first principle is that this truth is "self-evident." Yet history would suggest that it is anything but self-evident. Rather, history is a tapestry woven of countless stories of inhumane horrors. Neither is this confined to any one race, tribe, gender, or people group. It is this truth which must be continuously, intentionally, and uncompromisingly reiterated over and over and over again if it is to ever become self-evident.

Equally as epic in the document is the concept of the equality of humans as individuals. This was critical and fundamental not only for New World colonists in response to the British government but also for generations of Americans to come. The value of human life is not determined by country of origin, ethnicity, status in life or any other rank, but rather by the very nature of our shared humanity. This equality of every human must serve as a litmus test for all our beliefs and actions. That the United States almost immediately failed and historically repeatedly failed this litmus test in no way diminishes the importance of this principle and truth.

Like the ruby in the story, humans are the most valuable resource on earth; no other is comparable. By resource, we infer something of great value, endowed with rights and characteristics surpassing everything else in the physical world. A resource not to be exploited, traded, discarded, belittled, or coerced physically or mentally. It is, instead, a resource to which all dignity, respect, and honor should be ascribed. A value not attributed by virtue of its function but rather by virtue of its right. Yet history would suggest that such a view of humanity has seldom been the shared belief of any nation or people.

Like the vendors in the narrative, each of us has a variable value on human life based on our own experiences and personal beliefs. Shaped by biases resident within the respective societies or affinity groups in which we live and operate, the value of human life is, unfortunately, often a shifting concept that spans a spectrum. Fundamentally, this is at the core of most of the world's conflicts, both globally and locally.

Uniquely, the United States was founded on a recognition of the equal value of human life, and it has served as the cornerstone of the principles and character of the nation. In that sense, America was and is a "Great Experiment." What is of important note is that this unshakeable truth is most honored when exercised during the most difficult and turbulent times rather than the inverse.

In addition, humans are to be accorded certain rights: life, liberty, and the pursuit of happiness. Not only are humans the most valuable resource on earth, they have been granted certain undeniable rights. These rights prevent the exploitation of humans and help inform the proper form of governance for the people. A system of governance that protects life, insures liberty, and allows for the pursuit of meaning and purpose.

CHAPTER 7

The Trouble with Tribbles
A Study in Migration

*Remember, remember always, that all of us, and you and I
especially, are descended from immigrants and revolutionists.*

—Franklin D. Roosevelt

We asked for workers. We got people instead.

—Max Frisch

*A simple way to take measure of a country is to look at
how many want in . . . And how many want out.*

—Tony Blair

The US is currently experiencing the largest demographic
shift in its history. By all appearances, there is nothing whatsoever that can be done to prevent this from occurring.

Thus, we need to explore and understand the interre-
lationship between population growth, immigration, and
demographics. All three are closely related and, some would
argue, provide the impetus for true economic growth.

45

Population Growth

As of 2015, the world's population was at 7.26 billion. The top ten most populous countries are China, India, United States, Indonesia, Brazil, Pakistan, Bangladesh, Nigeria, Russia, and Japan. China (1.35 billion) and India (1.25 billion) are the only countries in the world that belong to the one billion population club. The US rolls in at a distant third place, at 321 million.

Currently, the birthrate in the US sits at 2.03 births per woman—a rate slightly below the replacement rate, which is 2.1 births per woman. Quite plainly, with regard to numerical births, the US is not currently replacing its existing population. There are a myriad of factors that have contributed to this marked decline in US birthrates including, but not limited to, economic prosperity, abortion, and racial and ethnic differences in birthrates. This is not unique to the US nor particularly among many developed countries. In Europe, the fertility rates are even lower, at about 1.3–1.5, and in Japan, at about 1.3. Historically, one of the most effective catalysts to bring down birthrates is significant and stable economic growth.

The world's population grew significantly in the 1960s, reaching the all-time high of a 2.1 percent annual growth rate in 1968. Some may recall that many apocalyptic scenarios were conceived for such significant growth. To provide a species of relativity, note that it is most probable that there were approximately 5 million people at the outset of the Neolithic Revolution, when humanity transitioned to an agrarian model of society. After several millennia, the world's population had grown only to somewhere around

200 million to 600 million by AD 1, representing a growth rate of about .05 percent per year—a snail's pace. It was not until nearly 1800 that we reached a world population of 1 billion. Within two centuries, by 1987, global population topped 5 billion. That said, growth rates since the late 1960s have been in steady decline. In 2015, the rate was 1.15% and it is predicted that it will continue to decline through 2050, at which time it could trough as low as 0.5 percent [Source: World Population Clock].

In 1979, Thomas Robert Malthus published *An Essay on Principle of Populations* and introduced the "Malthusian Trap." Malthus's thesis states, essentially, that the ability to meet the food demands of the world would not be possible, eventually resulting in a population check through starvation. That theory has proven to be incorrect due to human ingenuity and the development of agricultural technologies and efficiencies.

Of note is that this significant increase in population did not precipitate a decrease in the US's Gross National Product(GNP). Rather, the US GNP has been on a steady rise throughout this trending growth . . . right up to today, with only one drop occurring between 2008–2010—most likely an anomaly, reflecting the housing market crash and ensuing collapse of banks.

Given this inverse relationship, even in light of increased income and technological advances, it is clear that humans are and will continue to be an increasingly valuable resource. In fact, countries will not be building walls to stem the tide of this resource but rather competing for it. Why do we seem to be oblivious to a growing competition for human resources?

When in-country population replacement is not possible, immigration becomes necessary to reasonably sustain economic stability and growth. This makes immigration a topic of paramount interest, yet one so few seem to understand.

But what is the true story about American immigration? Are we truly a nation of immigrants?

Indeed.

There were numerous subsets of migrations to the United States[2], but for simplicity's sake, we will examine a set of ten waves of immigration—both forced and voluntary. The dates are approximations. These ten are not intended to comprise an exhaustive list, but rather to provide a baseline understanding of immigration in the US.

[2] Soerens, Matthew and Jenny Hwang, (2009) Welcoming the Stranger, Downers Grove, InterVarsity Press, 2009), pp.45-63.

Wave #1 (1492–1763): Spanish and English Colonists

While the Spanish were the first to settle in the United States, by 1650 the English established a dominant presence in the New World. Their first colony was in Jamestown, Virginia, in 1607, eventually resulting in thirteen well-established British colonies by 1770. Many of these early colonialists came to America fleeing religious persecution.

Wave #2 (1619–1860): African Slaves

While it could be argued that immigration should not include forced migration, it would be a dishonor not to acknowledge the 645,000 Africans who were forcibly brought to the United States. Slaves were first involuntarily transported to America in 1619 to the colony of Jamestown, Virginia, and continued to arrive against their will for nearly 240 years. The last known slaves arrived in the US illegally in 1859, on the schooner *Clotilde* to Mobile Bay, Alabama. They came in illegally because the transatlantic slave trade had been outlawed since 1808. The collateral impact of this inhumane period of American history is still being resolved to this day.

Wave #3 (1820–1860): Famine Irish and Revolutionary Germans

In the 1840s, Ireland experienced a devastating famine. This provided the impetus for many Irish farmers to migrate to the United States where they could secure farmland and begin anew. In the years following 1848, the United States saw significant growth in the number of German migrants. The Germans were leaving the governmental suppression of an attempted revolution by the people to create a national constitution with greater individual freedoms. The Germans left, seeking political rights available in the United States. This wave is a clear example of both the push-and-pull factors that have been an important part of the US immigration story.

Wave #4 (1848): Treaty Mexicans

Given current trajectories, sometime between 2045 and 2055 whites will no longer be the majority population in the US, and there will be no true majority population in the country. At that juncture, whites will be the largest minority population, followed by Hispanics. This should come as no surprise, given the history of Hispanic immigration or, in this case, naturalization to the United States. Mexican migrations over the years were often encouraged or initiated by the United States.

The Treaty of Guadalupe Hidalgo in 1848, which ended the Mexican-American War (1846–1848), secured for the US all or parts of what today make up California, Nevada, Utah, Colorado, Arizona, Wyoming, and New Mexico. Living on that vast territory were approximately one hundred thousand Mexicans who were granted US citizenship after they took an oath of allegiance. Those Mexicans can trace their ancestry back further than the early colonists to the United States. What currently makes up western or southwestern United States was at one time part of Mexico. This significant and relevant piece of our immigration history is often forgotten or unknown to many US citizens.

Wave #5 (1848–1890): Gold Rush and Railroad Chinese

Just days before the signing of the Treaty of Guadalupe Hidalgo, gold was discovered in California. It created waves of people seeking their fortunes in that State. Many of these earliest efforts required heavy recruitment to help mine the gold. Among those recruited were the "Chinamen" with promises of welcome and wealth. Most of the immigrants from China were men who, for the most part, came with the intention of making it big and returning to China.

For a number of decades, Chinese arrived first for the gold and then to assist in the construction of the Central

Pacific and Union Pacific railroads, completing the trans-continental railroad on May 10, 1869—seven years ahead of schedule. The building of the railroad was at no little cost in terms of human life. While no or few records were kept of the actual number of deaths, it is estimated that over one thousand people likely died in building the railroad.

Unfortunately, this wave of Chinese immigrants was to set a pattern for the way the US recruited immigrants in the future. A cycle ensued whenever cheap labor was required, exploiting and victimizing the recruits until they were no longer needed. After which, they were forced to return home or to remain under immigration legislation that prevented them from becoming naturalized citizens. In 1882, the Chinese Exclusion Act was passed by Congress and signed into law, preventing any new Chinese from entering the United States and preventing any Chinese already in the United States from obtaining citizenship. This Act remained in force until it was repealed in 1943.

It also provided the United States the opportunity to better understand the subsequent consequences, given the derivation of citizenship through birth in the United States for recruited immigrants. Recruiting immigrants without providing them with a pathway to naturalization inevitably creates endless challenges, particularly with regard to keeping families whole and intact.

Wave #6 (1880–1920): Italians, Polish, and Russian Jews

While the earlier European immigrants to the United States were predominately from western Europe, this new wave of Europeans were predominately native to southern and eastern Europe—primarily Italians, Poles, and Russian Jews. For the most part, these immigrants were processed into the United States through Ellis Island in New York, specifically those arriving after 1892.

The Poles migrated for a combination of reasons, many of which included Jews fleeing persecution in Poland. Polish immigrants came looking for economic opportunities and land ownership, given restrictions on both in Poland. Some of the German Poles also came seeking religious freedoms offered by the United States. The Poles often settled in industrial towns in the Midwest and mid-Atlantic States becoming steelworkers, miners, meat processors, and the like. This wave of Polish immigrants were predominately working class.

The Italians immigrated for economic reasons. Their farms had been divided into ever-smaller plots, making it all the more difficult to support themselves. This became increasingly true as global agricultural competition increased. Once in the US, they often would write home, encouraging others to join them, only further adding to the number of Italians leaving Italy. The heaviest migrations were derived from southern Italy.

The Jews in Russia left for religious reasons. During this time, they came under growing restrictions regarding where they could live, receive education, and engage in business—all of which was specifically outlined in the May Laws of 1882. The persecution of Russians Jews resulted in nearly one-third of the Jewish population migrating out of Russia. Many chose to come to America where they could find the religious freedom they were seeking.

It is estimated that some 23 million immigrants made the United States home from 1881–1920. This represented between 13–15 percent of the US population. It remains the largest percentage of foreign-born Americans at any time in the history of the United States. This large percentage of the non-natives, however, did not go unnoticed. Various groups formed to oppose the growing number of immigrants. Among those groups were the American Protective Association and the Immigration Restriction League of 1894. These groups utilized tactics very similar to the anti-immigrant tactics employed today—including redefining and renaming, often claiming the immigrants were illiterates, criminals, and madmen.

Wave #7 (1924–1965): Quota Migrants

Given the rather cyclic nature of US immigration history, it is no surprise that, following the largest wave of immigrants to the US, the response was to significantly slow or even stop the current immigrant populations from continuing to grow. The Immigration Act of 1924 did just that—by capping new immigration using census data dating back to 1890, thereby favoring northern European countries such as England, France, and Germany, while restricting southern and eastern Europeans, as well as Asians. It did not include restrictions on Mexican and Canadian immigrants as the southwestern states needed Mexican agricultural workers.

The Immigration Act of 1924 also introduced, for the first time in US history, the requirement that anyone entering the US do so with a visa. This new requirement ushered in the concept of "legal" and "illegal" immigration. Prior to 1924, migration was possible without any visa requirement. The oft-purported defense that "my ancestors entered legally," would now apply only if those ancestors arrived legally after 1924.

Wave #8 (1942–1964): Agricultural Mexicans

There was a growing demand for agricultural workers in the 1940s, especially given the shortage of workers caused in part by young men serving in the military during World War II and the corresponding growth in military jobs domestically. In 1942, the US and Mexican governments finalized a system which came to be known as the Bracero Program. In essence, this was a farm laborer program permitting Mexicans to enter the US as part of a guest worker program with temporary non-immigrant status. They were expected to return to Mexico at the conclusion of the farming season.

The program came under criticism from both sides given that it exploited the Mexicans both in terms of the living conditions accorded them and their respective wages. Conversely, it prevented US citizens from securing agricultural jobs given the program's contractual and cheap labor provisions. The "Bracero Program" lasted twenty-two years, until 1964, and it is estimated that more than 4 million Mexicans came into the US through it.

Wave #9 (1965–Present): Preference-Based Immigrants

It was time for immigration reform. The quota system had been in place for forty years and no longer addressed the immigration realities and needs of the country. Even more poignant was how the quota system reflected yet another example of the racial and ethnic discrimination that became prevalent during the 1960s. It was time for immigration reform that was not based on one's country of origin.

The Immigration and Nationality Act of 1965, enacted in 1968 (also known as the Hart-Celler Act), changed immigration to the United States in a manner that would address past challenges while, unfortunately, causing new ones. The intent of the Act was to grant preference to immigrants based on family ties in the US, as well as on job skills. The Act numerically restricted immigrants from the western hemisphere for the first time. It opened up greater opportunities for immigrants from Africa, Asia, and other parts of the world. Additionally, it created greater restrictions to Mexican other Latin Americans. Our current immigration system continues to operate under this Act, which is now nearly fifty years old.

Wave #10 (1990–Present): Undocumented and "Overstayer" Immigrants

In many ways, this tenth wave is a naturally occurring outcome of the preference-based immigration reform of 1965. It also explains why comprehensive immigration reform is absolutely necessary today. Regardless of where anyone stands politically, a careful study of our current immigration challenges makes it abundantly clear that our policies and systems need to be modified in such a manner that makes them responsive to the needs and realities of the twenty-first century.

Since about 1900 and up until 2007, the number of immigrants entering the country illegally or who overstayed their visas increased significantly from about 2.5 million in 1900 to nearly 12.2 million in 2007. Since 2007, that number has leveled off or decreased slightly. Of these immigrants, nearly 45 percent entered the country with a valid visa and simply did not leave when their visas expired. The other 55 percent entered the country without proper documents or illegally, and about half of them are Mexican.

According to our current immigration laws, to overstay your visa is a civil offense, and not a criminal offense. The severity of the crime, therefore, according to legislation, is akin to certain traffic violations, like running a red light, making an illegal turn, or having parking meter violations. This is a very important distinction and one not often understood by most US citizens. We quickly move from perceiving these actions as illegal, to labeling the individuals as illegal. Ironically, we do not apply the same principle to ourselves or others committing different civil offenses. That said, civil offenses do have penalties, and those penalties should be commiserate with the foible.

Since 1929, it has become a criminal offense to enter the U.S. illegally. It remains a civil offense to overstay a visa. Current immigration laws are, quite frankly, broken, and no longer serve the needs of the nation—neither the citizens nor the immigrants being welcomed. Now is the time for immigration reform, regardless of where you may stand politically.

What is very evident through these many waves of immigration to the US is that we are truly a nation of immigrants. We are not just European, we are African, Asian, Hispanic, Middle Eastern, and from every corner of the world. We span the globe in diversity, and that has been one of the differentiating attributes of America since the first western European colonists arrived. The US immigration story, however, does not end here. As evidenced in the chart below, we are on track to reach the highest percentage of immigrants in US history sometime around the year of 2030, at 14.8 percent.

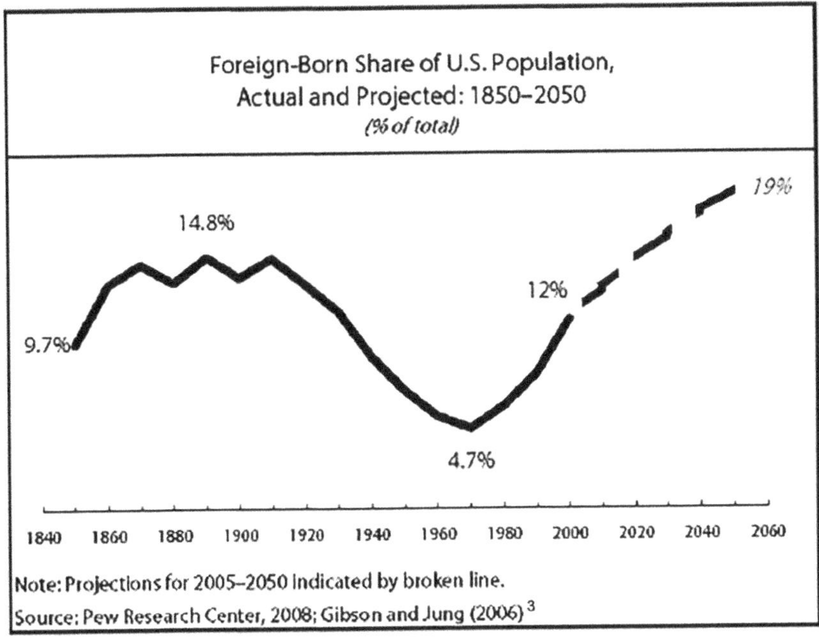

[3]"U.S. Population Projections: 2005-2050". Pew Research Center, Washington, D.C. (2008) http://www.pewhispanic.org/2008/02/11/us-population-projections-2005-2050/

The US has become great, not despite this diversity but more realistically because of it. It was not and is not the nation's military power that brought immigrants to the US, for they came long before America was a superpower. It was not, and is not, economic strength and stability, for they came here long before America was an economic giant. It was not, and is not, our academic institutions, for they came long before the US secured academic recognition. They came, and they still come, for freedom and for opportunity.

Do not confuse America's greatest asset with mirages, because without the nation's diversity, its magnitude in other areas would likely be significantly diminished. Closing the door on immigrants by creating endless lines that take decades to clear, with no lines for some, will make the country weaker and lesser on all accounts. It will rob the United States of its most fundamental value proposition . . . . the unmeasurable asset of American diversity.

CHAPTER 8

Convenient Diction and Dangerous Taxonomy

What's in a name? that which we call a rose

By any other name would smell as sweet.

—*William Shakespeare*

People are too complicated to have simple labels.

—*Philip Pullman, The Amber Spyglass*

When I'm born I'm black, when I grow up I'm black,
when I'm in the sun I'm black, when I'm sick I'm black,
when I die I'm black, and you . . . when you're born
you're pink, when you grow up you're white, when you're
cold you're blue, when you're sick you're blue, when
you die you're green and you dare call me colored

—*Oglala Lakota*

Throughout the course of human history, one of the most effective methods used in change dynamics consists of taking a commonly-used word with a well-established meaning and intentionally redefining the word so that its commonly understood meaning becomes a variant, evolving into a new definition. This can be accomplished by creating completely new meanings for universally used words. The practice can be engaged by any side or any angle on any issue. This practice can alter the meaning of a word to become more inclusive (incorporating individuals that may have otherwise been excluded). The word *marriage* is an example in modern society. Conversely, it can be done by narrowing the definition to be more exclusive. The word *baby* is an example in modern society. This diction adjustment can have positive ramifications, but it can just as easily become derogatory in nature.

One example in the past decade of this practice is the use of the word *amnesty*. Amnesty as defined by the *Merriam-Webster Dictionary* is "an act of granting a pardon to a group of individuals." Pardon as defined by the same dictionary is "excuse of an offense without penalty." The word *amnesty*, however, in the current vernacular has taken on a new meaning, intertwining itself tightly with the issue of immigration. Amnesty in the new vernacular is granting any pathway to legalization, even if a penalty is involved. Statements about amnesty no longer have anything to do with whether or not a penalty will be instigated.

Only eleven years after the Declaration of Independence was penned, and with it the principle that "all men are created equal," the Three-Fifths Compromise was enacted in 1787. Approved by the delegates to the Constitutional

Convention that year, the Three-Fifths Compromise allowed states to count blacks as three-fifths of a person in determining that state's representation in the US House of Representatives. In essence, this was a redefinition of equality—and an extremely pronounced one, at that. Essentially, one would have to surmise somehow that one and three-fifths were now equal. A similar three-fifths ratio was used as early as 1781 in the Article of Confederation for the purposes of determining national taxation. As ludicrous as this example may seem today, the practice continues.

A similar practice in change dynamics is replacing a commonly used word to rename something with a completely different word, often with an underlying meaning. This has been classically common practice with ethnic groups or nationalities. Nearly every nationality or ethnicity has been renamed with decretory seriousness and derogatory implications. The Dutch were once Dutchys or Cloggys. Germans were once Huns, Nazis, or Gerrys. Italians were Wops and Dagos. The English were Charlies and Limeys. These are simply examples on a very long list. This is true, we would venture, for every nationality or ethnic group around the world and is not unique to the US. These titles can also be expanded on to further define a specific group of individuals, for example, WASP (White Anglo-Saxon Protestant).

Sometimes, the endgame can be accomplished by simply adding an adjective and eventually dropping the original noun so that only the adjective remains. On the topic of immigration, one example would be "illegal immigrant" or "illegal immigration." The use of illegal immigrant has, in many ways, redefined both words . . . *illegal* and *immi-*

grant. It has almost become a normal paradigm to equate the immigrant, regardless of status, with being an "illegal immigrant." Yet, while there are various ways to enter the US legally and establish legal status, those facts are not what initially comes to mind for most Americans when the word *immigrant* is used. By definition, an immigrant is "a person who immigrates," and to immigrate is "to come into a foreign country and take up residence." In our fungible global society, people are moving to and from foreign countries regularly—taking up residency for business purposes, sports, the arts, and religious, political, or social reasons. In the US, a hopeful word has been transformed into something altogether nefarious.

Even more severe is reference to the word *illegal* in the US. Once solely an adjective, which is its proper function, it has morphed into a defining noun. The word is now commonly understood to identify immigrants who are in the United States illegally. The word *illegal,* in the American context, has all but become completely synonymous with *immigrants.* The term properly defined is "not lawful." Therefore, *illegal* applies to any act conducted, which is contrary to governing law. A traffic violation for example is not lawful, but we don't call traffic violators "illegals." This becomes even more muddled and complex on the immigration front when noting the difference between "improper entry" and "unlawful presence." Up to 45 percent of the undocumented immigrants in the US properly entered the country at one time, utilizing a visa, but simply stayed beyond the time limitations expressed in the visa. Thus, their continued presence here is unlawful, but, by definition, they entered the country lawfully.

Nomenclature tinkering often takes considerable time and effort, reaching a tipping point when words become common vernacular. But once critical mass is reached, they have the ability to catalyze stigma for generations. The power of words, and more importantly their meanings, cannot be underestimated. It remains very difficult to counter subversive efforts to redefine or rename people and groups. Often, it occurs when there is little or nothing that can be done to prevent it.

An additional condition about which the reader should be self-aware is the all-too-common aversion to alternative perspectives and arguments. Bigotry and intolerance are generally present in equal measure on both sides of any aisle, and more often than not, in greater measure amongst those who most loudly and often use the diction. This ironic intolerance defines a lack of self-awareness. Each of us are naturally drawn to that which we already understand, and can be evidenced by the polarization of the televised or printed news we choose to watch regularly, as well as a myriad of other things. This phenomenon will only further exasperate the current divisions within our nation.

Each of us, openly or subtly, believes that we fully understand the world in which we live and wonders whether the things we hear are true or false. Sadly, in many cases, the facts with which we are presented may be completely accurate but do not represent *all* the facts (the classic "sin of omission"). Thus, any honest attempt at interpretation and analysis will be necessarily biased. What any one of us knows is best represented by small segments of truth and falsehoods and far more generous areas of partial understandings and clouded perspectives that remain far from complete. This does not infer that others are lying to us with the intent to deceive; rather, it is our nature to make claims about truth based on what we believe to be true, but may be incomplete or even incorrect. The problem is not the obvious lie but the half-truth spoken in full confidence.

In order to weigh what we hear, perhaps we should consider requiring full disclosure from our sources of information. What are their biases? What is their worldview? Culturally, we have already determined full disclosure to be important enough for what we consume for nourishment, requiring all food products to include a complete list of ingredients and nutritional data. It would be logical to apply the same principle to our mental and ideological consumptions.

In the ensuing chapter, we will wrestle with specific ethnic and demographic challenges facing the United States of America. Before doing so, it is important to the authors to add a precursory caveat to the material ahead, in order to construct an appropriate framework with appropriate perspective.

Conveying unmitigated truth within this context must include what is, fundamentally, the most marginalized group in history, which would require its own volume to fully address the matter. The plight of women through the ages is the archetype for some of the dilemmas being unpacked here. A global culture of gender marginalization has carried itself from the earliest years of human civilization to our present hour. The paradigm of inequality between genders is something rooted so deeply in our collective psyche that it extends far beyond American borders, into more severe iterations that perpetuate themselves in endless cycles.

To be honest, the American marches and movements that openly dissent and denounce this problem are really only scratching the surface when they address visible manifestations such as inequality of compensation and other temporal problems, which are simply the fruit on a tree with deep and ancient roots stretching miles into its source. The problem is one that cuts to the soul of a worldwide system of beliefs. From majority cultures to minority cultures, there are few nooks and crannies where the marginalization of women is not the stuff of daily horror.

While the focus of this work is to a large degree, on the power shift occurring between races and ethnic groups in the US, it is very likely that we will simultaneously experience noticeable gender power shifts well beyond the scope expressed here. Such transitions will likely parallel and validate their counterparts.

Given the empirical shifts in contemporary American society, we need to be attentive to these realities. This is not an effort to conclusively resolve the stated challenges, as there are ancient practices in all societies—but rather to lay them plain within the framework of the current discussion. The intention of this chapter was to lift the veil so that we might understand, cease to perpetuate, and even prevent the subsequent harm that ensues.

CHAPTER 9

Bringing It Home
A Contemporary Status Report

Hispanics Misunderstood

> *Latinos are responsible for 29 percent of the growth in real income since 2005. They account for roughly 10 cents of every dollar of US national income, and that proportion is rising both due to growth in the Latino population and rising per capita earnings.*[4]

Hispanics comprise the largest minority group in the US at approximately 18 percent. Of note, Hispanics are not a racial group, but rather an ethnic group, inclusive of any race. The growth in the Hispanic population may give many non-Hispanic whites pause, but a brief review of US history is a quick remedy for the same. That history was addressed, in brief, in an earlier chapter. Those identify-

---

[4] Dr. Jeffrey A. Eisenach, Making America Rich Again: The Latino Effect on Economic Growth

ing themselves as white with Hispanic origin generally do not maintain the priorities many may perceive—immigration for instance. In fact, the two issues taking clear precedence within this population segment are education and employment.

Given that the Hispanic population currently has the highest birthrate among racial groups in the US, the areas of education and employment will be paramount in the years ahead. If the pattern continues, high birthrates will secure their place as the largest minority in the US.

It should give many non-Hispanic whites great comfort to know that Hispanics share very similar values with them, particularly in their prioritization of education and employment issues. The educational advancement of their children is a key priority to the Hispanic population. Hispanic parents actively endeavor for their children to surpass their own respective levels of education.

With the current problems associated with growing college debt and the burgeoning cost of higher education, it seems likely that Hispanics will be actively engaged in helping to find solutions to these challenges and the disparities within the nation's public education system. Hispanics have a vested long-term interest in seeing both of these educational crises fully resolved.

As it relates to jobs and the economy, the Hispanic community believes the impact of the housing crash and the ensuing recession in 2007 had a greater negative effect on their community than others in the US. The unemployment rates following the recession among the Hispanic population confirm this and particularly the fact that their unemployment rates rank higher than that of the general population. It should be noted that available data on the Hispanic population has, historically, been spotty at best. It is only beginning to receive the attention it warrants. Hispanics, however, remain optimistic about their long-term job and economic prospects. A strong work ethic drives this optimism, in no small way.

Black Lives Matter

> I'm hoping to dismantle the public notion—for folks outside of the community—of what Black Lives Matter means. It's really about saying that black lives matter, that humanity is the same when you go inside people's homes.[5]

The year 2016 demanded the attention of America, as the media highlighted police shootings of several African American men throughout the US. The shootings resulted in unnecessary deaths, and many of the video recordings of the incidents were broadcast for public scrutiny and collective analysis.

Thus was birthed a movement that became best known as "Black Lives Matter." The shootings and the Black Lives Matter movement generated immense public attention and countless perspectives and positions from all sides. If this movement remains active, it will undoubtedly generate ongoing dialogue and further action. Regardless of your position on the matter, viewing that footage raises import-

---

[5] *Ava DuVernay in an interveiw by Michael O'Connell with Oprah Winfrey and Ava Duvernay for The Hollywood Reporter on August 17, 2016*

ant questions that warrant further investigation and ongoing dialogue.

Unfortunately, this is not unique to 2016. Although events may have been more prolific and certainly more publicized, they have been boiling over for years. This dilemma is indicative of a far greater issue. Profiling to facilitate searches, arrests, and incarceration has been rampant for decades.

The complexity of these issues are, without question, immense. Is this a nationwide issue or localized? Do the videos provide us with the full context of the events, or only the necessary or unnecessary conclusions? When should lethal force be used? Were events escalated, rather than diffused? What role does mental health play in such events? What role does racism play? What about the epidemic of black on black violence? Have we turned to trial by the masses or reality-television justice? Will mandatory police video cameras put an end to the root causes of this issue? The list goes on.

This chapter is not a response to the complexity of these events but rather an acknowledgment of how they further validate the premise and thesis of this work. All racial, ethnic, and social classes will increasingly expect their voices to be heard. They will demand either a change in the power structures of the country to address the issues or a modification of those power structures to prioritize them.

What has become evident to many is that having elected an African American president did not secure a pathway for significant change. Sadly, unrealized expectations only exasperate these issues and cause many to become even more disillusioned with our current political system. Many more African Americans may choose not to vote in coming elections, as it has not proven to be an effective instrument of change.

What then has historically moved issues important to the African American community forward? History would suggest community action in the form of protest, civil disobedience, and even violence have more effectively served to call attention to these matters. This is not an endorsement of those forms of engagement, but rather a review of the historic reality and a warning to be heeded.

Issues prioritized by the African American community, as well as almost any community, do not resolve themselves. The strength and validity of an argument does not drive functional change. Those pieces are necessary but only the inception of a process. These societal conundrums require concentrated efforts to realize lasting and productive change. The catalysts giving birth to the Black Lives Matter movement are not going away, nor will they be brushed aside. They will, indeed, continue to demand the nation's attention.

The Art of an Apology

> *WHEREAS my eyes land on the statement, "Whereas the arrival of Europeans in North America opened a new chapter in the history of Native Peoples." . . . Yet I'm serious when I say I laugh reading the phrase, "opened a new chapter." I can't help my body. I shake."* [6]

---

[6] *Layli Long Soldier poet and member of the Oglala Sioux Tribe from her book WHEREAS*

Public Law 111-118 was signed into law on December 19, 2009, by then President Barack Obama during his first year in office. Also known as the Department of Defense Appropriations Act of 2009 or HR 3326, it still may not ring any bells for most readers. Nevertheless, it was important to one group of Americans.

Defined as "An Act. Making appropriations for the Department of Defense for the fiscal year ending September 30, 2010, and for other purposes," this legislation is an interesting study in policy-driven reconciliation and reparation. What is notable here is the section included under "other purposes." Included here is the relevant portion Section 8113, also titled "Apology to Native Peoples of the United States."

> [7]Section 8113: (a) Acknowledgment and Apology.—The United States, acting through Congress—
>
> (1) recognizes the special legal and political relationship Indian tribes have with the United States and the solemn covenant with the land we share;
>
> (2) commends and honors Native Peoples for the thousands of years that they have stewarded and protected this land;
>
> (3) recognizes that there have been years of official depredations, ill-conceived policies, and the breaking of covenants by the Federal Government regarding Indian tribes;
>
> (4) apologizes on behalf of the people of the United States to all Native Peoples for the

many instances of violence, maltreatment, and neglect inflicted on Native Peoples by citizens of the United States;

(5) expresses its regret for the ramifications of former wrongs and its commitment to build on the positive relationships of the past and present to move toward a brighter future where all the people of this land live reconciled as brothers and sisters, and harmoniously steward and protect this land together;

(6) urges the President to acknowledge the wrongs of the United States against Indian tribes in the history of the United States in order to bring healing to this land; and

(7) commends the State governments that have begun reconciliation efforts with recognized Indian tribes located in their boundaries and encourages all State governments similarly to work toward reconciling relationships with Indian tribes within their boundaries.

> (b) Disclaimer.—Nothing in this section—

> (1) authorizes or supports any claim against the United States; or

> (2) serves as a settlement of any claim against the United States.

When is an apology truly an apology? When does an apology, in and of itself, warrant another apology? Is it time to hit reset? Yes. How about working toward true reconciliation and an effort to bring healing to our land? A sincere act of this nature must be as public and collective an act as possible to be even remotely effective.

If the treatment of Native American peoples has taught America anything, it should be the fact that the relegation of any segment of society to second-class citizenship will inevitably create generational cycles and long-term challenges that negatively impact everyone. This apology demonstrates just how little we understand how to extend a true apology. But we can learn from this foible and persevere. America needs healing, and there is no better place to begin than with those who protected this land for centuries before any other immigrants claimed it as their own.

Whitewashing Asians

> *On The Great Wall: We have to stop perpetuating the racist myth that a only white man can save the world. It is not based in actual fact. Our heroes don't look like Matt Damon. They look like Malala. Gandhi. Mandela . . .*[8]

According to recent census data, the fastest-growing racial group in the United States is the Asian population. While the Asian population comprises about 6 percent of the total population, it has, interestingly, surpassed the Hispanic growth rate. This spike is, however, due not to prolific birthrates but rather migration.

---

[8] *Constance Wu tweeted on July 29, 2016*

The Asian American population deals with a unique set of issues that are, nevertheless, discriminatory and racist, in nature. These respective issues are generally given little, if any, attention and often require intentional research to be analyzed and understood.

The Asian American population is in no way monolithic, but is often perceived and treated in this manner. For many Americans, it is as if all Asians came from one homogeneous location. This monolithic treatment of Asians is evidenced in many ways, but perhaps most notably in the diversification plans of colleges and in the workplace.

Any number of labels have been employed to define the Asian American population. They include, for instance, the "invisible race" and the "model minority." This renaming process is further expounded in a previous chapter of this work. These names, however, don't necessarily reflect the life experiences of many Asian Americans.

The diction and bigotry driven through this particular brand of renaming, however, is a phenomenon bolstered by a long history in Hollywood and the general media. More recently, it has been reignited, and is known as "whitewashing." This occurs when Asian roles in Hollywood movies are played by white Caucasian actors. This practice goes back many years to an Asian American with universal recognition—the immortal Bruce Lee. Lee's acting career was negatively impacted and, subsequently, curtailed due to racist concerns about casting an Asian in lead roles. Particularly offensive and ironic is the fact that, in real life or in fictional representation of the character, they were originally Asian. Astounding.

The existence and scope of the whitewashing issue is not a widely understood phenomenon. But, in 2016 alone, there were over ten movies in which whitewashing was prevalent, including the casting for *Doctor Strange* and *Ghost in a Shell*. Further inclusions are *Power Rangers*, *Whiskey Tango Foxtrot*, *Spider-Man Homecoming*, and *The Great Wall*. While some may argue there are far more serious issues to address, it is that perspective that further exasperates the plight of the "invisible race" and contributes to its sustained obscurity.

The inevitable redistribution of power within American society will take on many faces. Often, the methodologies required to address the power shifts will be somewhat reflective of the cultural norms and traditions of the respective ethnic groups directly involved. In the case of Asian Americans, such efforts will most likely be through a medium of legal recourse. Lawsuits and advocacy to change or create new laws will naturally be the option of choice, rather than public protest or unrest. This approach, however, in no way diminishes the significance and importance of these issues within the Asian American population segment. "Invisible" and "model" titles may actually serve them well when securing desired changes within the system. That is not to say, however, that a few "angry Asians" will not also be effective in calling attention to a collective cause that warrants our attention.

CHAPTER 10

Shifting Sands
The Redistribution of Power
in American Society

Let us never forget that government is ourselves and not an alien power over us. The ultimate rulers of our democracy are not a President and senators and congressmen and government officials, but the voters of this country.

—*Franklin D. Roosevelt*

I do not deny that I planned sabotage. I did not plan it in a spirit of recklessness nor because I have any love of violence. I planned it as a result of a calm and sober assessment of the political situation that had arisen after many years of tyranny, exploitation and oppression of my people by the whites

—*Nelson Mandela*

The fact that the United States is undergoing the largest demographic shift since the wave of European colonists stepped foot on these shores is fairly common knowledge.

With each successive national census, the day when whites will no longer be a majority becomes ever closer and ever clearer. Current estimates place that majority-minority point of critical mass somewhere between 2045 and 2055.

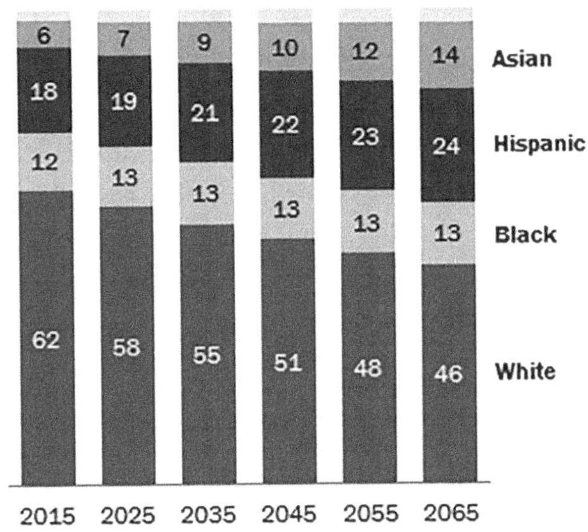

By 2055, the U.S. Will Have No Racial or Ethnic Majority Group

% of projected U.S. population

Note: 2015 numbers are estimates; numbers for other years are projected. Whites, blacks and Asians include only single-race non-Hispanics. Asians include Pacific Islanders. Hispanics are of any race. Other races shown but not labeled.

Source: Pew Research Center projections

PEW RESEARCH CENTER [9]

[9] "By 2055 the U.S. Will Have No Racial or Ethnic Majority". Pew Research Center, Washington, D.C. (2017) http://www.pewhispanic. org/2015/09/28/modern-immigration-wave-brings-59-million-to-u-s-driving-population-growth-and-change-through-2065/ ph_2015-09-28_immigration-through-2065-17/

During the school year 2014–2015, at a national level, non-Hispanic whites were no longer the majority for K-12 students in our public school system. Wow. The reality is that American children are encountering this shift first and are adjusting to it accordingly. Subsequent generations of children will grow up in this diverse context. Hopefully, this will occur with more than simply an acceptance of its reality but rather with a true appreciation for it.

Adults are still getting used to the idea. For many, although it may be a foggy realization on the fringes of distant future, the reality of the dynamic has not yet completely hit home. That said, there is an ever-burgeoning flow of articles, books, blogs, and public discussions on the subject. Rightfully so! This inevitable demographic change has ramifications for our country that require collective awareness and appropriate navigation. Thus, the focus here is not so much about the demographic shift itself, but rather the corresponding power-change dynamics that will necessarily follow such a phenomenon. The reality of the shifts are not only evident in our public school system and in large urban centers, but also in communities across the country that may have been historically predominately white or African American.

Yet another metric supporting this shift is in the number of biracial or multiethnic families in the United States. In 2013, 12 percent of newly married couples were interracial. Interracial marriages impact far more people than solely the nuclear family. The extended families of the individuals are also influenced by these unions. Additionally, children adopted from other races or ethnic groups play into the overall model.

Estimating the Size of the Multiracial Population

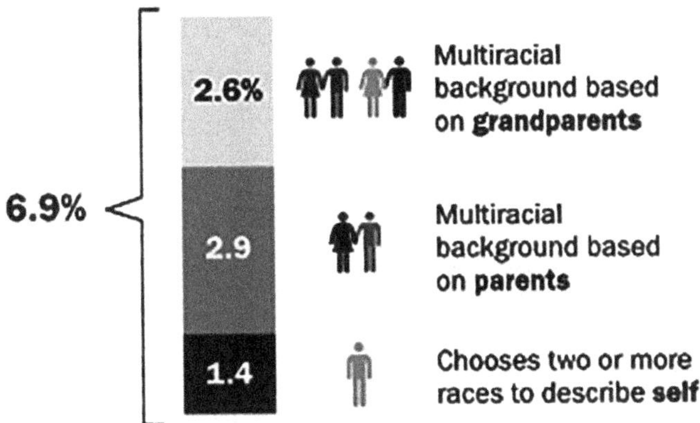

Respondents can be counted as multiracial one of three ways:

First (**self**), if they select two or more races for themselves.

Second (**parents**), if they do not select two or more races for themselves but report that at least one of their biological parents was not the same race as them, or select two or more races for at least one of their parents.

Third (**grandparents**), if they do not fit the definition of multiracial based on their own or their parents' racial background, but indicate that at least one of their grandparents was not the same race as themselves or their parents, or select two or more races for at least one of their grandparents.

Source: Pew Research Center survey, Feb. 6-April 6, 2015 (n=21,224 sampled adults)

PEW RESEARCH CENTER[10]

---

[10]"Estimating the Size of Multi-Racial Population". Pew Research Center, Washington, D.C. (2017), http://www.pewresearch.org/fact-tank/2015/06/11/how-pew-research-conducted-its-survey-of-multiracial-americans/st_2015-06-11_multiracial-americans_00-02/

The population segment most fundamentally impacted by this tsunami are, and will continue to be, those who have historically identified themselves as white Americans. Unfortunately, within the white community, such dynamics are often addressed in an unconstructive and even harmful manner. A subconscious gravitation toward affinity and social comfort, as well as a conscious manifestation of fear, work together to make tackling the issue particularly difficult.

The success of Donald Trump in the political forum did not occur in a vacuum. It is the result of several factors, and this work would be remiss to attempt to attribute it to a single issue. With that in mind, the issues addressed in this book added to the fertility of the ground in which Trump's candidacy sprouted. Quite frankly (and again, this book remains an apolitical examination of real events, not an analysis of their merits), Trump's presence is undeniably a reaction by a significant segment of the white population. He particularly resonates with those who are struggling with the demographic power shifts they sometimes observe and, more often, sense surrounding them. This segment lives with a certain level of uncertainty and anxiety about America's future. What does whiteness mean in this new world?

This progressive transformation, however, will not be limited only to the white population. It will, in fact, impact each and every ethnic population in the US. Since 2001, Hispanics have become the largest ethnic minority. Subsequently, the dynamic between the African American and Hispanic populations warrants further analysis and study. How does a growing Asian population within the US play into the equation, particularly given their ever-increasing representation within the business and academic sectors? Quite simply, there is not a racial or ethnic group that will not be impacted in some manner by this change.

The growing momentum of the current Black Lives Matter movement is a viable example of how racial and ethnic communities will respond to these changes in American society. Already poised with a strong and burgeoning voice in media, sports, and other esoteric spheres of influence, minority populations will increasingly engage opportunities to address prejudices and injustices that may have previously been ignored or simply not realized nor considered by the majority population. The current process is simply the beginning stages of what will eventually mature into a growing number of respective movements and idealistic challenges to American society. Issues associated with the failure of our public education system, the impotency of our incarceration system, and inadequate representation in the arts and politics are but a smidgeon of what will be addressed openly in ensuing years.

How America responds now and in the next few years will determine the tone, severity, and ramifications of these societal transitions and the United States' path forward. Although the country has shined and excelled on many levels, handling a shifting ethnic and cultural landscape has not been America's forte; and as history has taught us, we should fully anticipate reasonable differences in regional responses. Reflecting on some of the most enlightened, progressive, and influential perspectives in history, we can, perhaps, extrapolate insights that will aid us.

In *The Republic*, Plato states, "Constitutions cannot come out of sticks and stones; they must result from the preponderance of certain characters which draw the rest of the community in their wake." The 2016 American election cycle has demonstrated this truth in a truly bipartisan manner. Ultimately, those leaders rise who can best surmise and articulate the deepest concerns, relevant at any point in time, of those they claim to represent. Often, their stated positions are a thing of shock and awe to much of the populous who were unaware of underlying issues and subsequently run the risk of responding in anger and rage, and meeting with the same. This catalyzes greater division and ultimately fails to address the fundamental cause of the issue or issues at hand. Plato further conveys various iterations of states, with democracy being one of them, rife with inherent flaws like all others. Democracy can, ironically, readily lend itself to despotism.

Historians through the ages—not unlike Plato or Montesquieu in his *The Spirit of the Law*, or even James Madison and Alexander Hamilton in *The Federalist*—all recognized the importance of the separation of powers and the concept of checks of balances. They came from differing perspectives and views and leaned one way or another, but the core of their values were consistently similar. Each recognized the importance of creating infrastructure wherein power was distributed carefully between varying groups, ultimately to prevent the abuse of great power.

John Emerich Edward Dalberg Acton, better known as Lord Acton (1834–1902), was a prominent British historian. In one of his letters to Bishop Mandell Creighton in 1887, Acton wrote, "Power tends to corrupt, and absolute power corrupts absolutely." Power, whether insignificant or absolute, requires the establishment of succinct controls that permit the necessary exercise of power while limiting it inherently.

Any constituency will allow leaders to amass significant power, particularly in the midst of the unknown and impending fear, real or imagined. However, that power will ultimately be checked if it infringes on the freedoms of other members of society. Social and civil revolution is an inevitable outcome of pushing the envelope too far, and many leaders through history have explored those boundaries. In his work *Great Political Thinkers: Plato to the Present*, William Ebenstein writes, "History is a vast graveyard filled with self-styled 'realists' like Napoleon, William II, Hitler, and Mussolini. They all underestimated the important imponderables in the equation of power and missed, in particular, the one component that in the end proved decisive: the will of man to be free, to put freedom above all other goods, even above life itself."

Martin Luther King Jr., in his *Letter from a Birmingham Jail*, wrote, "My friends, I must say to you that we have not made a single gain in civil rights without determined legal and nonviolent pressure. History is the long and tragic story of the fact that privileged groups seldom give up their privileges voluntarily."[11] Such a statement strikes at the core of what may result from the demographic shift currently underway in American society. If privileged groups are not prepared to give up the privilege of power afforded to them by a majority status within a democratic system of governance, it seems that history teaches us that natural forces will apply a level of pressure to force those changes. As previously noted this also risks a change in the Republic system of governance, itself.

[11]Martin Luther King, Jr., 'Letter from Birmingham City Jail', in *A Testament Of Hope: The Essential Writings Of Martin Luther King, Jr.,* ed. James Melvin Washington (San Francisco: Harper & Row,1986), 292.

CHAPTER 11

Kairos Moments
Responding to Demographic Realities

*That men do not learn very much from the lessons of history is
the most important of all the lessons that history has to teach.*

—Aldous Huxley

Throughout its history, America has experienced
"nation-changing" moments that have shaped the country
in monumental ways. Clearly, the American Revolutionary
War and the Civil War are two of the best known kairos
moments in our collective past. Their outcomes defined
the trajectory of our corporate narrative. But there are
other events that have also contributed to American history—a myriad of decisions, actions, and reactions—woven
into our current context.

Without question, one of the defining factors about
America is its progressive nature and willingness to change.
A significant aspect of America's strength comes from its

84

remarkable ability to synergize a wide array of diverse cultures, comprised of a unique collection of ethnicities and affinity groups.

Estimates of the United States population at the middle of the twenty-first century vary, from the UN's 404 million to the US Census Bureau's 422 to 458 million. To develop a snapshot of the nation at 2050, particularly its astonishing diversity and youthfulness, we will use a round number of 400 million people.

The United States is also expected to grow somewhat older. The portion of the population that is currently at least sixty-five years old stands at 13 percent, and is expected to reach about 20 percent by 2050. This "graying of America" has helped convince some commentators of the nation's declining eminence. For example, an essay by international relations expert Parag Khanna envisions a "shrunken America" lucky to eke out a meager existence between a "triumphant China" and a "retooled Europe." Still, though, America maintains a relatively high fertility rate compared to parts of Europe or China; the number of children a woman in the US was expected to have in her lifetime peaked at 2.1 in 2006, with 4.3 million total births, the highest levels in forty-five years, thanks largely to . . . you guessed it . . . immigration. Immigrants tend to have more children than residents whose families have been in the United States for several generations. Moreover, the nation may be on the verge of a baby boom, when the children of the original boomers have children of their own.

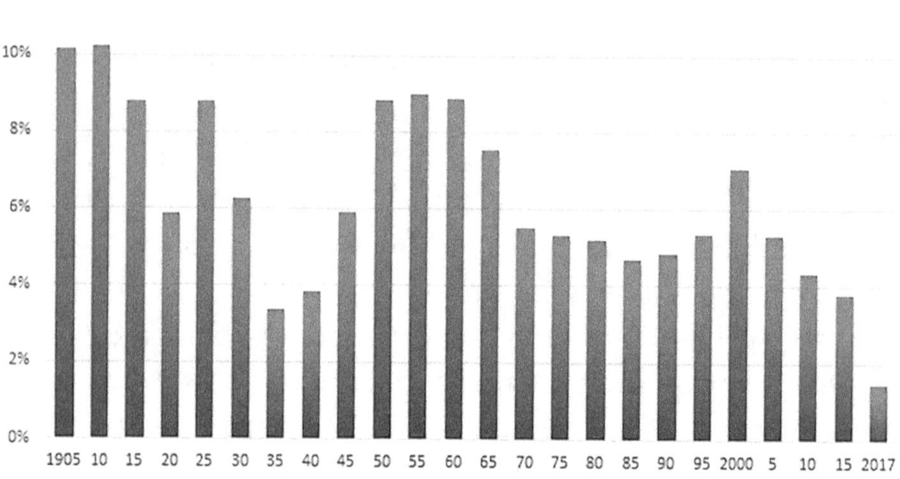

[12]Source: Russell Baril using U.S. Census Bureau population estimates

Between 2000 and 2050, census data suggest, the US fifteen-to-sixty-four age group is expected to grow 42 percent. In contrast, because of falling fertility rates, the number of young and working-age people is expected to *decline* elsewhere: by 10 percent in China, 25 percent in Europe, 30 percent in South Korea, and more than 40 percent in Japan.

The prospect of an additional 100 million Americans by 2050 worries some environmentalists. As noted in this work, many have joined traditionally conservative xenophobes and anti-immigration activists in calling for a national policy to slow population growth by severely limiting immigration. Many would purport that Americans who favor larger families are not taking responsibility for "their detrimental contribution" to population growth and "resource shortages."

Such critiques do not seem to take into account that a falling population and a dearth of young people may pose a greater threat to the nation's well-being than population growth. A rapidly declining population could create a society that doesn't have the work force to support the elderly and, overall, is less concerned with the nation's long-term future.

Immigration needs to continue to be a major force in US life. The United Nations currently estimates that around two million people a year will move from poorer to developed nations over the next forty years, and more than half of those will come to the United States. In 2000, according to the Organization for Economic Cooperation and Development, an association of thirty democratic free-market countries, the United States was home to 12.5 million skilled immigrants, equaling the combined total for Germany, France, the United Kingdom, Australia, Canada, and Japan.

If recent trends continue, immigrants will play a leading role in our future economy. Large American firms are also increasingly led by people with roots in foreign countries. For all these reasons, the United States of 2050 will look different from that of today: whites will no longer be in the majority. The US minority population, currently over 30 percent, is expected to exceed 50 percent before 2050. No other advanced populous country will see such diversity.

With recent and upcoming shifts in American demographics, we are assured that change is afoot. Precisely what that change will look like remains to be seen, but it is an inevitable, rising tide that will carry our nation into the twenty-second century. This is a kairos moment—a rather thin period where economic and political power will begin to evolve naturally according to the organic processes and subsequent composite changes the nation's experiences. While many fear these changes will be detrimental, in fact, nothing could be further from the truth.

In addition to the necessity to stay ahead of the birth-rate curve, a dynamic our immigrant population drives forward is the provision of labor at a competitive rate. While at first glance this comment may seem antithetical to the argument, it is in fact central to the value of most waves of immigration, historically, and is no less relevant today. As in days past, there remains the need for a labor class that fills a gap in the economic structure by allowing the US to remain viable in specific industries, both domestically and abroad.

The simple fact of the matter is that Americans who are established laborers, willing to work hard to make things better for their families, are simply not able to engage the lowest level of agricultural and other labor-centric vocations at a rate that allows them to provide for their families, and permits those industries to continue to exist and even thrive in a competitive global market.

While it may sound somewhat draconian in nature, the role that immigrant labor has played and continues to play in American society is a large part of Adam Smith's "invisible hand" working on our behalf and the reason certain industries are not forced to pay a closer-to-median wage within a constrained fiscal model, which, frankly, would simply drive them out of business. Immigrants fill this role, and the first and second generation of immigrants to any wave flowing into the US is generally more than willing to spend significant time in this context, establishing their financial base and driving their overall standard of living up slowly over time.

In almost all such cases, the economic situation and general standard of living those immigrants experience in the US is much superior to their country of origin. Thus, all parties win; and rather than labor being stolen from the multigenerational American, he or she is able to pursue a more viable and generally specialized type of labor at an overall bump due to the continuity of other industries within the nation. We are able to keep companies and even entire economic sectors open due to this phenomenon, and we owe it to the periodic influx of immigrant laborers who, unknowingly, save some of the more primal and cost-challenged economic entities within our overall purview.

Thus, we can conclude with even just these two arguments that continuous immigration into the United States is not just a historical reality but a beneficial necessity to the nation. It keeps us poised, keeps us centered, and keeps us competitive in an increasingly tighter global community, with a movement toward greater parity each day. Without this infusion, the future would hold a much greater level of uncertainty.

In effect, America whispers these words to its immigrants as they pass through the portals of our nation and prepare to engage a labor force that longs for their impetus:

> Do not let the hero in your soul perish, in lonely frustration, for the life you deserved but never have been able to reach. Check

your road and the nature of your battle. The world you desired can be won. It exists, it is real, it is possible, it is yours.[13]

---

[13] Ayn Rand, John Galt in *Atlas Shrugged*

CHAPTER 12

No Man Is an Island

No man is an Iland, intire of itselfe; every man

is a peece of the Continent, a part of the maine;

if a Clod bee washed away by the Sea, Europe

is the lesse, as well as if a Promontorie were, as

well as if a Manor of thy friends or of thine

owne were; any mans death diminishes me,

because I am involved in Mankinde;

And therefore never send to know for whom

the bell tolls; It tolls for thee.

—John Donne

The immortal words of John Donne are no less true today than they were in 1624, not long after the Pilgrims landed at Plymouth Rock. Yet even the ageless and sage advice offered to us in *No Man Is an Island,* is not sufficient to lead us to anything resembling a universal understanding of humanity's symbiotic nature and the sheer power to change the face of the planet that such an understanding would bring to mankind.

Isolationism is the policy or doctrine of trying to isolate one's country from the affairs of other nations by declining to enter into alliances, foreign economic commitments, or international agreements, and generally attempting to make one's economy entirely self-reliant—seeking to devote the entire efforts of one's country to its own advancement, both diplomatically and economically, while remaining in a state of peace by avoiding foreign entanglements and responsibilities. In centuries, even decades past, this approach to world affairs may have actually had positive utility. The early nineteenth century in the US as well as the post-Depression period of late 1930s both marked a time when the state of the Union seemingly required an adherence to a policy of isolationism, and the matter can be argued historically.

Unfortunately, we do not live in 1805, or 1935, or any other period of history when the world was not tied together through technology, massive social networks and instant communication gateways, as well as through the globalization of economic realities and military implications. No longer will a "Josey Wales," Western loner style of interaction and governance, have any relevance in our collective purview. Gone are the days when we more easily ignore injustice or make decisions internally without external consequence.

More fundamentally a question might be whether it remains appropriate to stay silent and absent even when we are fully aware of the ills and horrors surrounding us. To answer a question accurately, one must take it to minimal extreme and maximum extreme to test its viability. If you, assuming you are of a reasonable age to engage this publication, were to walk out of your front door and view a five-year-old bashing the head of a three-year-old against the sidewalk in front of your house, what would you do? Most likely you would run out, grab the five-year-old, pull him aside with one hand, and, with the other hand, attend to the toddler. Why would you do this? There is but one reason. You possessed power and an understanding of what was right and were able to juxtapose your power with your understanding and create an ethically appropriate outcome.

You did not know the five-year-old, the three-year-old, or anyone else related to them. The property under the sidewalk does not belong to you but rather the city and is maintained through public works. You have no stated policies pinned into your lawn regarding laws governing how children should and should not behave. Quite simply, the ethical conclusion is simply self-evident because it is an example whose immediacy cuts across Kantian absolutism and John Stuart Mill's utilitarian views as well. They simply cease to contend with the severity of the moment. This may be interpreted as a supportive assumption for Just-War Theory, but it is rather, in this case, a microcosmic paradigm for how any entity with power is responsible at some level for those without the power to protect themselves—both at home and abroad.

Why? Life is precious. Yes. Because the act was horrific? Yes. But most importantly is the fact that you possessed intrinsic power, and with that power came an intrinsic responsibility to act justly, and to save the three-year-old. Moving this model to a macrolevel is not really a complex transition. The ethical implications apply, albeit the practical application is not always as easy to engage, or even surmise.

At a secondary level of logic, the economic factors relevant to the discussion are fodder enough to challenge any move toward isolationism. The world grows smaller by the day economically; and while the United States may raise its exports and lower its imports, and, thus, improve the health of its economic equation . . . the very nature of the equation itself becomes more relevant to the nation's need to take an inclusive approach to the affairs of the world, and reject isolationism.

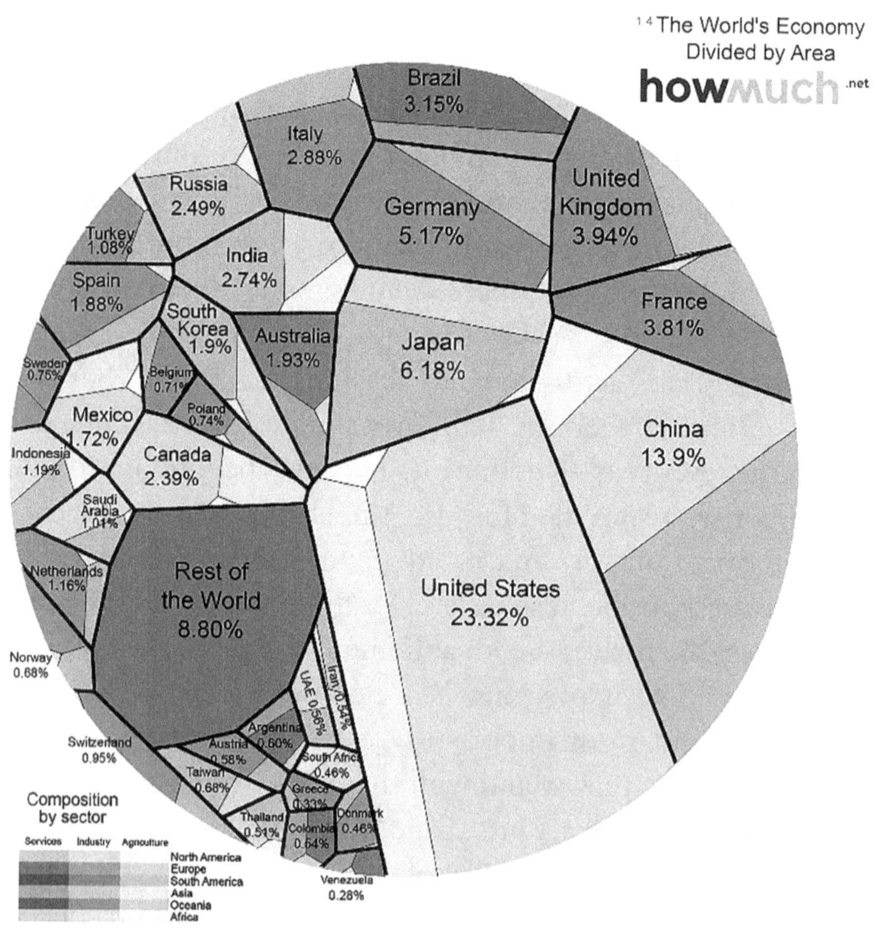

We are moving toward a global economy. One way of approaching that is to pull the covers over your head. Another is to say: It may be more complicated—but that's the world I am going to live in, I might as well be good at it. (Phil Condit, Former Chairman and CEO of Boeing)

I find that because of modern technological evolution and our global economy, and as a result of the great increase in population, our world has greatly changed: it has become much smaller. However, our perceptions have not evolved at the same pace; we continue to cling to old national demarcations and the old feelings of "us" and "them." (Dalai Lama)

This present window of opportunity, during which a truly peaceful and interdependent world order might be built, will not be open for too long—We are on the verge of a global transformation. All we need is the right major crisis and the nations will accept the New World Order.[15]

The way of the isolationist is the way of the Dodo. Closing borders and operating in a lone-wolf manner is simply not a reasonable answer to the complexities that exist in the world today. The United States is, for the most part, a remarkably well-balanced system of governance and economics. It maximizes personal and public freedoms through a republic-based constitutional model, and maximizes personal economic utility through true private ownership and rewards for producing economic stimulus. This separates us from systems, whether better or worse, that do not provide these same utilities.

---

[15] *David Rockefeller*

CHAPTER 13

Social Epiphanies and Their Butterfly Effect

The Scorpion was hamstrung, his tail all aquiver, Just how would he manage to get cross the river, "Why, the water's so deep," he observed with a sigh, which pricked at the ears of a tortoise nearby.

"Well, why don't you swim?" asked the slow-moving fellow, "Unless you're afraid, I mean what, are you yellow?"

"It isn't a matter of fear or of whim," said the scorpion, "But that I don't know how to swim."

"Ah, I didn't mean to be glib when I said that, I figured you were an amphibian."

"No offense taken," the Scorpion replied, "But how about you help me to reach the far side? You swim like a dream, and you have what I lack, what's say you take me across on your back?"

"I'm really not sure that's the best thing to do," said the Tortoise, "Now that I see that it's you. You've a less than ideal reputation preceding, there's talk of your victims all poisoned and bleeding. You're the Scorpion, and how can I say this, but well, just don't feel safe with you riding my shell."

*The Scorpion replied, "What would killing you prove? We'd both
drown, so tell me, how would it behoove me, to basically die at
my very own hand, when all I desire is to be on dry land?"*

*'The Tortoise considered the Scorpion's defense. When
he gave it some thought, it made perfect sense. The
niggling voice in his mind he ignored, and he swam
to the bank and called out, "Climb aboard."*

*But just a few moments from when they set sail, the Scorpion
lashed out with his venomous tail. The Tortoise too late,
understood that he'd blundered, when he felt his flesh stabbed
and his carapace sundered. As he fought for life he said, "Tell
me why you have done this, for now we will surely both die?"*

*"I don't know!" cried the Scorpion, "You never should trust
a creature like me, because poison I must. I'd claim some
remorse or at least some compunction, But I just can't help
it, my form is my function! You thought I'd behave like my
cousin the crab, But unlike him, it is but my nature to stab."*

*The Tortoise expired with one final quiver, And then both of them
sank, swallowed up by the river. The Tortoise was wrong to ignore
all his doubts, because in the end friends, our natures win out.*

*Soooo, what can we learn from their watery ends? Is there
some lesson on how to be friends? I think what it means is that
central to living a life that is good, is a life that's forgiving.
We're creatures of contact. Regardless of whether we kiss or
we wound, Still we must come together. Though it may spell
destruction, we still ask for more, Since it beats staying dry, but
So Lonely on shore. So, we make ourselves open, while knowing
full well it's essentially saying, "Please, come pierce my shell."*

—David Benjamin Rakoff

Stepping Out, Stepping Up, and Leading the Way with Trust and Forgiveness

Throughout life, we learn to protect the things around us that we value: our families, our possessions, and ourselves. On multiple levels, this is the fruit of sound nature and nurture, meeting a primal instinct to survive and to sustain that which we cherish. Unfortunately, that same self-preservation drips into other areas of our lives and creates puddles, pools, lakes, and oceans of self-preservation protocol, which is not quite so healthy, and in fact detrimental and counterproductive to our original intentions.

The fable of the scorpion and his fateful river crossing is well-known and is generally an example of our inability to change our basic inclinations and fundamental natures. In that context, there is a measure of hopelessness it catalyzes in each of us. But we would contend that the lesson it teaches is more in line with Rakoff's modern interpretation of the ancient tale.

The pivotal issue is rather our willingness to step out of our comfort zones to help others, even when we are uncomfortable with them. In the case of the tortoise's moral dilemma, he paid a price for the decision. Nevertheless, was the decision wrong? He chose to trust. He chose to serve. He chose, in fact, to love. Albeit he vetted the logic of mutually assured destruction as part of his thesis for the decision, he still chose to take a chance and traverse the moral high road that could, and did eventually, cost him greatly.

The stakes and personal liabilities we are addressing in this book are hardly that of the tortoise. Yet, more often than not, we choose self-preservation and distrust while we entrench ourselves in the safety of our temporal cocoons, barring the proverbial door to others for fear of loss, fear of harm, and fear of anything else that might give us discomfort. On some level, this is wisdom; but when taken to its logical extreme, it is a virus of selfishness that breeds bigotry, fascism, and a myriad of other global maladies that are epic in nature and nearly impossible to rectify.

The significantly underrated film *Cloud Atlas* (which can only be appreciated after its fourth or fifth viewing) captures the ethos of social responsibility in a uniquely existential manner. While its level of complexity is difficult for many to grasp in one sitting, much of its philosophical premise is remarkably poignant. David Mitchell, author of the novel that catalyzed the film, provides thoughtful commentary throughout his work. Note a selection from one of the films chronological periods.

> *The Revelation of Sonmi 451: To be is to be perceived, and so to know thyself is only possible through the eyes of the other. The nature of our immortal lives is in the consequences of our words and deeds that go on and are pushing themselves throughout all time. Our lives are not our own. From womb to tomb, we are bound to others, past and present, and by each crime and every kindness, we birth our future.*

Mitchell's inclination toward reincarnation theory may be suspect and has little bearing on the current discussion, but his understanding of personal responsibility outside of ourselves is profound. He essentially puts hands and feet to

Donne's *No Man Is an Island* and challenges us to examine, not only our personal perspective on social responsibility, but also what we have done to contribute to the condition of the world around us. A perpetual butterfly effect of outcomes is at work with every decision we make related to how we treat others.

To distill this concept into its most primal context is to understand the second mandate of Jesus's Golden Rule, "Love thy neighbor as thyself." Thus this discourse might seem overly simplistic at some level. It is not. It is, in fact, one of the most profound statements and subsequent personal revelations in the course of history. It is the fundamental change agent and Rosetta Stone for world peace.

Sadly, we are all scorpions at heart. Even the most noble among us is not exempt from some species of self-protective bigotry and unrighteous judgment. If it were not so, the simple truths above would be employed and practiced much more universally, and the world would look quite a bit differently than it does today. That is not the case, though, and we are each dealing with our own personal demons of this nature in some manner or another.

What then can be done as it relates to the condition of our nation today? This chapter has propounded a basic concept that every reader, save the rare sociopath, understands and embraces. It is no great epiphany, to be sure. The key, then, is to begin with the tiniest of steps—just a smidgeon of adjustments. The first is to understand our part in the universal butterfly effect and to truly embrace the fact that we can make a difference.

Armed with this perspective, we begin to change. We begin to understand who our neighbor is and what our responsibility is to our neighbor. Our neighbor on another continent or our neighbor next door. Geography does not dictate the nature of our neighbor but rather by something much, much more fundamental. Our neighbor is not defined by ethnicity or gender or wealth or lack thereof. Nor is our neighbor defined by our cultures and the vast differences between them. Our neighbor is defined by our common humanity.

In the United States, this realization will result in a number of revelations and potential paradigm shifts. That which is different from us is not to be feared—nor even tolerated. It is eventually to be celebrated but certainly at the outset of our journey to simply be "understood."

Whom do you fear? Who is your "bad guy"? Pick one close to home. Whom do you fear? We could choose gentler nomenclature; but at the core of the matter, the jokes we tell in private, the bigoted perspectives that leak out of our mouths and into our children's ears are all driven by fear. And there is no single population segment who is more or less guilty than any other. We mock that which we fear, and it overflows from even the most reserved soul, if the poison resides there.

Begin to identify who your "bad guys" are. For the majority white populace in America, it is often whichever minority group is most prevalent in their respective region. But make no mistake, everyone has a bad guy. As individuals and as groups ascending in concentric circles, we all adopt our own personal nemeses. Who are yours?

CHAPTER 14

Who's Your Bad Guy?

Whatsoever therefore is consequent to a time of war, where every man is enemy to every man, the same consequent to the time wherein men live without other security than what their own strength and their own invention shall furnish them withal. In such condition there is no place for industry . . . no knowledge of the face of the earth; no account of time; no arts; no letters; no society; and which is worst of all, continual fear, and danger of violent death; and the life of man, solitary, poor, nasty, brutish, and short.

—Thomas Hobbes

One of the most common foibles of the human condition is our inexhaustible ability to live myopically within our own failings and misperceptions while ever retaining an astute ability to see them in others at a glance. This is, at some primal level, a coping mechanism to allow us to live within our own worldview and justify the beliefs and subsequent behaviors that we individually proliferate. Nevertheless, it is at its core a failing of mankind and a major contributor to every conflict in history. Is there a way to break free from such fetters?

Clearly embracing this simple understanding is a first step to reaching outside of our own iron circles to see ourselves and the world as we truly are. One of the manifestations of this condition is our individual and collective tendency to choose nemeses. Generally "different" than us and our affinity group in some manner, our nemeses take on many shapes and sizes; and most deny having them all the while.

Who is your nemesis? This excludes a disdain for individuals and groups with truly nefarious ethos, i.e., "I detest people who murder others," or "I cannot tolerate people who lie for their own gain." This is not the species of internal animosity being identified here. Rather, it is that which we have toward others who, when you really break it down, are not doing anything wrong, other than being different and acting in a way that is not "our way."

Everyone has a bad guy. One of the authors of this publication grew up on the East Coast in a county north of the Baltimore metropolitan area. Rural in nature and predominately white, there was animosity toward African Americans. They were close by, perceived as an urban threat, and diverse enough from rural culture that they were the enemies of choice. There were no Mexican or American Indian or Jewish or Catholic jokes growing up. There were jokes about black people. Awful, horrific jokes.

The interesting thing was, while growing up there, there still existed a minority group of blacks in the county and, for the most part, no one in the schools or even socially would openly engage these racial perspectives. In certain areas of the South, this is not the case where there is more cultural allowance for outspoken bigotry, but not in this county of Maryland. Instead, it was a passive-aggressive disdain, where one might say, "One of my best friends is a black guy," if conviction were pressing, while telling a joke ten minutes later.

The same author moved to a city just northwest of Denver during his college years, and the sentiments were quite different. There were lots of black people around, but they raised almost no ire in the white population, and there was very little, if any, bigotry toward them even subtly. Instead, it was the Mexicans. Yes, indeed, every ill in the region was conceived by the majority of whites to be catalyzed by Mexicans—of which there were no small number. In this context, the bad guy changed because the differentiating minority group changed.

A close friend from Wisconsin, during a similar discussion, stated that in his region of Wisconsin, there were almost no African Americans, Hispanics, or any minority groups to speak of. It was a haven of white America and variances in culture were confined to which Lutheran church you attended. So what to do? In his area it was "Those people from Illinois." Drivers from Illinois would regularly descend on that area in droves for vacations and other reasons, and the animosity toward them was fierce amongst the natives.

The point of these examples is to demonstrate that each of us, individually, and our affinity groups, culturally, have villains we create. They are the brunt of jokes, the cause for discomfort on public transportation, and the cause for many perceived ills and inconveniences affecting us. And make no mistake, it is not simply a phenomenon confined to the majority group within a population. The minority groups often have strong angst toward those who outnumber them—a result of their status in the social structure and the very human response they have to it.

Thus, one of the first steps in shifting the winds that are driving the ethnic tensions within our nation is to, at the very least individually and preferably collectively, recognize whom we are busy hating. That may be a strong word, but when you boil it down, it is hatred that drives such sentiment and behavior. To own it, is to begin to purge it.

Ponder your own context. Is there a specific group that gets you riled up? Perhaps there are even empirical reasons you maintain, which justify your position. A higher crime rate than your affinity group. A lower median income than your social group. A lower level of education than your peer group. We craft a narrative of hatred, however subtle and deniable—born of reasons of all shapes and sizes—in our hearts; and we nurture our children into the same worldview. It is inevitable.

If there is any hope at all for us to turn the tides of racism, which have washed over the nation, the inception to the cure can only be realized by changed hearts. One heart at a time has to change. Reminiscent again from David Mitchell's thoughtful commentary in *Cloud Atlas*:

> *My life amounts to no more than one drop in a limitless ocean. Yet what is any ocean, but a multitude of drops?*

How true it is. It is certainly the reason we vote and make our civic efforts within the republic in which we live. A next step might be translated into a personal effort to recognize our biases toward others and to counteract them with kindness, forgiveness, understanding, and eventually love.

CHAPTER 15

The Thousand-Mile Journey

*"So I say to you, my friends, that even though we must face the
difficulties of today and tomorrow, I still have a dream. It is a
dream deeply rooted in the American dream that one day this
nation will rise up and live out the true meaning of its creed—we
hold these truths to be self-evident, that all men are created equal.*

*I have a dream that one day on the red hills of Georgia,
sons of former slaves and sons of former slave-owners will
be able to sit down together at the table of brotherhood.*

*I have a dream that one day, even the state of
Mississippi, a state sweltering with the heat of injustice, sweltering with the heat of oppression, will be transformed into an oasis of freedom and justice.*

*I have a dream my four little children will one day live in a
nation where they will not be judged by the color of their skin
but by the content of their character. I have a dream today!"[16]*

—Martin Luther King Jr.

[16]Martin Luther King, Jr., *'I Have a Dream'*, in *A Testament Of Hope: The Essential Writings
Of Martin Luther King, Jr.,* ed. James Melvin Washington (San Francisco: Harper &
Row,1986), 219.

MLK's *I Have a Dream* speech is common fodder for most high school and undergraduate public speaking courses, as a bastion of other areas of sociological study. Dr. King's approach to the racial problems in the United States were not unique; but they were rarely so well-articulated, analyzed, and addressed with strategy for action that reflected immense wisdom and character. Dr. King saw that solidarity could be leveraged and productive if it remained consistently peaceful. His mission, vision, and values drove a catalyst for change that has, arguably, been unmatched in its relative scope since his assassination.

The work you are reading admittedly examines a wider array of social injustice than simply race, but regardless of the malady being addressed, the message remains the same. Cease judgment and harm; increase acceptance and goodwill. Unfortunately, the most simple of messages, while poignant, often have a more difficult time percolating into the human soul, and true change at the cultural level is a seemingly unsurmountable climb.

Lao Tzu, Chinese founder of Taoism, stated, "The journey of a thousand miles begins with one step." Tzu's admonition here is simply that it's difficult to get something significant done, but unless you forge into the effort from the ground floor, it will never happen. Put another way, the most difficult aspect of conquering any task, or social ills in the case of our examination, is believing things can change, and then subsequently that we can, individually, do anything that would make an impact.

Hopefully, reading this book has given you some perspective regarding the fact that things *need* to change . . . but also helped you understand that things *can* change.

Because they can. But only if enough people care to make it happen. For each of us, the first step of the one-thousand-mile journey is to realize that the journey can be engaged and completed. Armed first with that understanding, rooted soundly in our souls, can we finally begin to make both the internal and external adjustments to our personal lives, to our personal perspectives, and to our communities.

This book is not meant to be an instruction manual for solving America's angst, but rather an effort to remove the veil from the eyes of the beholder and bring each reader a step closer to self-actualization. It is meant to change worldviews and to shine a bright light into our own hearts and minds to seek out the hidden places where we contribute to the problems. An opportunity to be honest about the dark places in ourselves and to commit to transforming them.

There is no quick fix for the problems we have examined. There is no leader who will solve them for us, nor mantra that will universally summarize their resolution. True change begins internally; and its outworking, inevitably, affects the external. Simply "doing things" that are good and logically counteractive to collective hatred and isolationism will not truly solve these problems. We each need to understand that our beliefs, our biases, and our supposed social adversaries are passed down to our children and are reinforced in society each moment that we adhere to them. Doing good deeds has its merits, but learning how to love others is better. The good deeds will come unconsciously when we are transformed internally.

But how do we change ourselves and the way we think so that we can change the world. Nothing happens overnight, but as expressed in the previous chapter, pinpointing our own biases and contributions to the malady is a place to begin. After that, it's a straightforward matter of good old-fashioned self-awareness. When we identify a dose of bigotry cropping up, we will feel its talons because we have unveiled its nefarious nature. When we feel fear and distaste of other cultures within our country, whether close by us or across the country, we will know its sickness still needs to be inoculated.

Action will follow. Of significance, one of the best actions, far surpassing attendance at a rally, casting a vote, or giving financially to a good cause, is the model we provide to those around us. Inevitably, the concentric circles of relationships in our lives—from those closest to those we barely know—will be impacted most significantly by observing and being exposed to internal change in others. A myriad of noble activities will help, but the handful of epiphanies we generate in the hearts of others will eclipse them.

All of this is not to say that taking action is not beneficial. It is simply imperative to understand that action, be it social policy change or government programs or a wealth of other systemic adjustments, have not and will not fix the problems we face. This is evidenced throughout our history and in every nation around the globe for as long as humans have engaged organized civilizations. The primary reason for this is that corporations often use guilt and shotgun type approaches to organizational dilemmas that may provide short-term promise, but rarely result in long-term resolution. Additionally relevant, is the fact that the very need to implement these types of things is a glaring recognition of the fact that we have collectively done little of our own accord, and are now attempting to slap a bandage on visible cuts and scrapes, when there is a deep cancer abiding in the body.

So . . . if we change the way we think, and do not keep it a secret from those around us, will we have done enough? Absolutely not. But understanding what actions and activities are true game changers, and which are a waste of time, is key to understanding how we should expend our labors and precious time.

We propose that the most poignant and effective tool for external change in society is the act of reconciliation. Stated simply as the "restoration of friendly relationships" in most dictionaries, reconciliation is in fact the most powerful key to driving both internal and external change.

CHAPTER 16

Reconciliation
Forging a Path through the Desert

*The weak can never forgive. Forgiveness
is the attribute of the strong.*

—*Mahatma Gandhi*

*Forgiveness is the fragrance that the violet
sheds on the heel that has crushed it.*

—*Mark Twain*

A work of this nature demands practicum. It naturally lends itself to reflection, analysis, paradigm change, and finally pragmatic action. What then should those actions be? Before dealing with the endgame, it is vital to note that the human terrarium in which we navigate our brief terrestrial experiences is wrought of more than sticks and stones. There are significant metaphysical and, if you like, spiritual realities that are vital to charting an appropriate course ahead within the societal problems here explored.

Monumental wounds run deeper in groups than they do in individuals, and the healing process is just as monumental an undertaking. Of vital importance is understanding that the key to moving forward, with any hope of success, is based on forgiveness and reconciliation. Testifying to this phenomenon are the countless ongoing regional conflicts that are held at bay for seasons and unleashed at intervals with furious terror, often unexpectedly. Throughout Africa, the Balkan States, the Middle East, and a myriad of other regions around the globe, deep animosity brews for generation after generation. Why?

The fact of the matter is that peacekeeping efforts in these areas are only skin-deep remedies that temporarily stave off genocidal activities, which would be employed by any number of the opposing parties if given the opportunity. Many of these bastions of hatred are centuries old; some have existed for millennia. Each successive generation is taught, from cradle to grave, precisely who their bad guy is, and precisely how evil that bad guy was, and could be again. Like the proverbial boogeyman in the closet, the nemeses born of ethnic and cultural clashes provide the fodder for a species of, albeit sick and depraved, commonality around which an esoteric society or affinity group can rally and remain intact and cohesive.

In such situations, can peace ever be reached? Indeed it can.

Take for instance, the case of Germany. The oppressive force driving two world wars within just a few decades, there was no shortage of reasons for nations and people groups throughout Europe to harbor a deep hatred of the German people to this day. But that is not the case. And while the world will always keep a wary eyeball on any effort to resurrect a modern German war machine, given the conquering and dominant nature of the nation, it harbors no tangible anger toward Germany and has moved on.

Now, is this because Germany has provided fiscal utility for the union of nations it once conquered less than a century ago? Absolutely not. It is, rather, because Germany was repentant for its crimes. It owned its sins against millions of Jews and Gypsies and citizens of Allied nations and other groups, and came to the world forum afterward, rife with guilt, asking for forgiveness. In fact, an unnecessary layer of guilt still pervades the nation today.

The power of forgiveness at work, however unmeasurable and unfathomable and mystical it may or may not seem to you, is as real at a macrolevel as it is between two individuals. Understanding this phenomenon is key to understanding the Rosetta Stone for our own internal tensions. Similar to Rwandan, Congolese, Balkan, or Syrian genocidal hatred, the same root of bitterness is the vein from which our own national tensions flow.

Today there are just a handful of Native Americans in the US. At one time, they were a populous group of people inhabiting vast stretches of land. The grandchildren of European immigrants wiped them out—hunted them down like dogs in the late nineteenth century and rounded up the last few to relegate to the worst pieces of land on the continent. The fact of the matter is that there are not enough Native Americans around to make enough noise to be a significant social force in contemporary American culture; but the reality of past actions is not excused by their numbers.

Not so with African Americans. Comprising over 12 percent of the population, they have a voice, and at times are given more attention. After four hundred years of slavery, they suffered for another century under segregation and rejection, especially in certain parts of the country. While the federal government attempted to address the worst of it in the midsixties, the schism between the sons and daughters of slaves and the sons and daughters of slave owners remains quite pronounced. If anything, tensions are higher than ever.

Such problems cannot be addressed by reparations alone. Neither casinos on reservations nor subsidies for college-bound minorities will fix these problems. The act of reconciliation is our only true hope to see fundamental and lasting change. Reconciliation is defined as the restoration of friendly relations. Quite simple really, but impossible without forgiveness. Whether Native Americans or African Americans or any other group that has suffered at the hand of the majority (generally white, male) population in America, there will be no true progress or peace without forgiveness.

So what needs to happen? Well, the answer is straightforward but not easy. The sons and daughters of those slave owners and Indian killers need to identify with the "sins" and misdeeds of their ancestors, acknowledge those specific offenses, and ask forgiveness. It *does not matter* that it did not happen during your generation. The wound remains festering and open; and the only ointment is identification, ownership, and humbly asking forgiveness of those who have been wronged.

What does this look like? A nationally televised event with the most significant white leaders of the day recognizing the wrongs their ancestors perpetrated against the ancestors of another group?

Yep. That's what it looks like.

But that probably will not be the first step in this process, and the pragmatic majority of the population will likely scoff at the idea that anything so far removed from current realities would have any existential value. This is evidenced by the Department of Defense Appropriations Act of 2009. Nevertheless, this is how true change can and may come one day. It has proven itself to be the only recipe for success, and its absence is proven in multigenerational genocides throughout the ages.

But this book is not so much a call to petition leaders for an act of corporate reconciliation, as it is an effort to help readers understand what is taking place around them and what the true remedies for the dilemma are. At the end of the day, we are truly only responsible for that which we can do personally. If the reach of our activities and choices can be extended to a wider impact in society, then our responsibility is increased, commiserate with the knowledge we possess. But the scope of most of our realities is constrained to our locale and our finite relationships.

Without reconciliation and true forgiveness, real change is a farce. Peace can be tacked up like a veneer over the problems at hand, but it will not be achieved at a fundamental level until the ointment is applied to the wound. One hundred years from now, the same angst today will perpetuate itself in some new manner unless the inevitable tide of hatred and angst is subdued.

In truth, apathy is the agent that pervasively blankets and clouds the minds and hearts of the apparently unempathetic segments of society. It is not so much the fact that most individuals cannot conceive of and intellectually understand the need to recognize the value in others and the subsequent need to begin to embrace them as "neighbors."

It is also not so much the fact that most individuals are mean-spirited and harbor a nefarious intent toward anyone outside their purview (though we all know a few). No, indeed. It is rather the plain and simple fact that most folks simply do not care enough, or at all. The pressures of busy lives and the deafening roar of more immediate demands drowned out the quiet but persistent awareness that the world, while shrinking, is still much larger than the scope of what we survey and perceive within our finite spheres of existence. Certainly, large contingencies of enlightened and socially conscious individuals gravitate toward a proactive reckoning in this context, but they are a minority, and often still in need of self-evaluation themselves, having come to decisive and immovable conclusions on some matters. The much wider, detached populous comprises the change catalyst necessary to stop, think, decide, prioritize, and begin grinding the flywheel to a halt.

Are you a part of that group? Are you a casual observer of injustice, attending to your own affairs, but passing on the other side of the road when inconvenience trumps empathy? Everyone is guilty in varying degrees, and progress on this path is the steepest footpath of our one-thousand-mile journey.

CHAPTER 17

Tsunami Averted
A Call to Action

Be the change that you wish to see in the world.

—*Mahatma Gandhi*

All segregation statutes are unjust because segregation distorts the soul and damages the personality. It gives the segregator a false sense of superiority, and the segregated a false sense of inferiority.[17]

—*Martin Luther King Jr.*

[17]Martin Luther King, Jr., 'Letter from Birmingham City Jail', in *A Testament Of Hope: The Essential Writings Of Martin Luther King, Jr.,* ed. James Melvin Washington (San Francisco: Harper & Row,1986), 293.

Quite frankly, there is no easy fix for any problem of significant magnitude in any society or culture, barring cataclysmic necessity. The media and press have the national ear and the ability to drive collective epiphany, but they have been, for the most part, impotent in their efforts, quite frankly, driven by their own biased ends, as well as oblivious to many of the general realities in recent decades. It is with this in mind that we draw our work to a close with a call to action. How could we do otherwise?

But talk is cheap, and lists of action steps that will never be engaged are useless. Pragmatism is in order to bring closure, and that will be the fundamental approach to the conclusion of this discussion. In initiating closure, it is appropriate to convey a well-known parable in the Bible, told by Jesus. It is presented with changes (in bold).

> *And Jesus said to him, "What is written in the Law? How does it read to you?"*
>
> *And he answered, "You shall love the Lord your God with all your heart, and with all your soul, and with all your strength, and with all your mind; and your neighbor as yourself."*
>
> *And He said to him, "You have answered correctly; do this and you will live." But wishing to justify himself, he said to Jesus, "And who is my neighbor?"*
>
> *Jesus replied and said, "A man was going down from* Phoenix *to* Tucson, *and was* carjacked, and robbed by locals outside a convenience store where he had stopped, *and they stripped him and beat him, and went away leaving him half dead. And by chance a* conservative Christian pastor of a large church who was late to a meeting *was going down on that road, and when he saw him, he passed by on the other side. Likewise a* professor outspoken on social justice issues from a large university *also,*

when he came to the place and saw him, passed by on the other side. But an illegal Mexican immigrant lady, *who was on a journey, came upon him; and when* she *saw him, she felt compassion, and came to him and bandaged up his wounds, pouring oil and wine on them; and she put him on her own beast, and brought him to an inn and took care of him. On the next day she took out two denarii and gave them to the innkeeper and said, 'Take care of him; and whatever more you spend, when I return I will repay you.' Which of these three do you think proved to be a neighbor to the man who fell into the robbers' hands?"*

And he said, "The one who showed mercy toward him."

Then Jesus said to him, "Go and do the same."[18]

The point of this story is not to pick on conservative pastors or socially liberal professors, nor to suggest Mexican immigrants have an inherent inclination to behave better than their named counterparts. That is a nonsensical interpretation. Rather, as was Jesus's intention, this story lays plain the thing that really matters . . . that is, how we treat one another when no one else is looking. True love for our neighbor is not a respecter of persons. In the paradigm presented, the lowest tier of society acted in the highest manner, making her and her actions superior on several levels to others in the tale. The true measure of a citizen's value is what lies in his or her heart and how he or she treats others

---

[18] *The Holy Bible, Luke 10:25-37*

within the society—more so than what they can produce, earn, or offer practically.

We can only hope this work has served to awaken the reader to some of the changes that are at work in the US and, more specifically, how the redistribution of power among the citizens of this country has the potential to become even more disruptive. Subsequently, we hope that we have made clear how this dynamic drives impending danger to our republic.

A review of America's historic responses to similar power shifts gives us ample fodder from which to learn. In doing so and examining the virtues and vices of previous national activities, we hope this work will provide a platform for virtuous responses moving forward. Our best years as a nation can be, and hopefully are, before us. Those years will not be great without effort or without a collective understanding of how not to repeat past mistakes. It will require effort and constraint and patience, and at times, it will be excruciatingly painful. There is no microwave-ready solution for success. Victory in this effort will require a recommitment to principles and values that have been clearly articulated throughout our national history and the more expansive history of all of human civilization.

A willful and thoughtful metamorphosis can only be achieved through open dialogue, necessary engagement of divisive and tense issues, and a willingness to understand we may be wrong about certain things we have classically held true. Let us be careful not to confuse a lack of tension and honesty with a passive-aggressive peace. True peace is achieved through a crucible of honesty, conflict, tension, and a burning desire for justice.

The question for many will be, what can I, as an individual, do about it? Far more than you may think. It, however, must begin with you. You independently increase the possibility that we collectively will respond appropriately and effectively to every issue that has been addressed. We will each need to commit to be part of the solution and not to fuel the problem, mutually exclusive from the choices and actions of any other human being.

The most practical, simple, and initial step in this journey is a willingness to commit to learning about other people: the way they live, the way they think, and the reasons they do so. Logically, the most effective and leveraged approach would be to perform this analysis on those with whom you relate most seamlessly. This would encompass those within your own race, affinity groups, ethnically, economically, and culturally. Their apples have not fallen so far from your tree that you cannot surmise the nature of their variances and perceived foibles more readily. Choose those within your own affinity group who think or act in ways that continually surprise you, with whom you disagree, and whom you do not understand.

It has become remarkably evident that there are segments of society that are completely polarized ideologically, although they coexist in matching affinity groups. The art of listening, then listening some more, and eventually understanding the wellspring of their perspectives will be essential to this process.

Evaluate each situation unabashedly and without emotional investment, and ask questions about anything and everything that vexes you, shocks you, or befuddles you.

Do not jump to conclusions. Ask questions. Here are a few to consider:

> What is it, specifically, about the behaviors and beliefs I am observing that impact me, either positively or negatively?

> What do I know about this person's background that may affect the behaviors and beliefs I observe?

> If I were in this person's shoes, knowing what I know about their life and their background, how would I feel? What would I do?

> Do I feel threatened in some way by this individual or his/her affinity group because of a power shift in society or some other perceived or real threat to my life, livelihood, loved ones, or personal values, which I can surmise?

> Have I placed this person in a neatly labeled box? Have I renamed their affinity group? Why did I do it, or why did I allow myself to embrace the view of others?

> Did my immediate family and my peer group shape my perspectives about this person at an early age? What did they say about this person's affinity group?

> Is there valid data to challenge my views?

Thus far, the exercise provides the impetus to perform analysis. It has not been consummated but simply defined by a protocol of empathetic evaluation. Ensuing stages will allow us to surmise the more severe and potentially detrimental perspectives to which we adhere.

With the process of empathetic evaluation in action, identify your bad guy(s). As stated, we all have a bad guy. It may take some thoughtful processing with the list above to surmise them, but it won't take long. It is not a collective exercise but rather one which must be engaged individually. Others may provide some measure of input or supplement your conclusions, but this is your reckoning in the deepest and most honest crevices of the heart. Who's your fall guy? When all else fails, who can you blame for many of the ills in society? Surprisingly, this is often those most similar in nature to you and not the inverse. For those most poignantly attuned to ethnic and cultural variances, it will generally be individuals who disagree with their intrinsic ideologies. These maladies of bias are often the most difficult to address, because the supposedly enlightened are often averse to evaluating ideological variances, having themselves overcome the more basic and obvious bigotry they have previously identified and currently pontificate.

Learn more about your bad guy. What is it that makes them so bad? Be specific. The more concisely we articulate the nuances of disdain and distaste, the better will be our ability to overcome our myopic natures. Do so through the empathetic filters previously employed. Test what you believe is true. Engage this effort personally rather than vicariously, and engage the group or individual in some manner on a personal basis. This might be accomplished by volunteering or by visiting a specific neighborhood for lunch or simply by striking up a conversation on public transportation. Eat their food, listen to their stories, and try to understand their joy and pain. Learning in this manner requires proactivity and effort, but it is a priceless exercise. Internal change does not come easily.

As an ancillary supplement to these activities, we each should learn about our own immigration story. Unless you are a full-blooded Native American, you are the product of some species of American immigration within the confines of recorded history. Most likely, this is empirical information that you can access. Engage your parents, grandparents, and extended family members. Discover your ancestry. It may not be what you think. You might be quite surprised by the results.

Additionally, watch or listen to at least three different news stations with varying perspectives. Read about the same report in three different news publications and compare what each has to say about the situation. Determine how the same situation can be reported from such different perspectives. Where is the truth, or does each contain part of the truth? Rather than approaching the process with predetermined conclusions and hardened perspectives, divorce yourself from your own soapbox and enjoy the exercise as a clinical study of sorts. Assume that what is being presented is not a conscious effort to deceive, but rather an honest effort to convey from a completely different worldview and set of ideologies.

An integral part of the change dynamic juxtaposed with an unencumbered perspective and increased level of empathy is the adoption of certain behaviors and habits that are necessary to sustain a healthy evolution in this regard. The art of listening cannot be overstated. This includes listening to those with whom we have already determined we do not agree, as well as those for whom our first inclination is to reprove or rebuke. Listening quietly and not talking over them—but rather allowing them the opportunity to explain their position and perspective—is a key element in our ability to engage effectively.

Appropriate protocols for listening to and understanding others are learned behaviors. They build on one another and will be unnatural to those unversed. Nevertheless, they are essential to every aspect of life.

1.) Practice extending common courtesies and kindnesses. Address people politely, welcoming them. Ask if you can assist others or simply greet or acknowledge them.

2.) Add knowledge to your kindness. Know those groups identified as your "bad guy." Ask yourself what specifically you dislike or fear about them. Discern what you currently know about them and determine if it's true or if it may only be true for a small number. Do not rely on esoteric sources for knowledge. Seek out several.

3.) Add self-control to your knowledge. Not everyone will be as knowledgeable as you about certain subjects or people groups. Thus, you will need to extend to others the grace, the time, and, perhaps, the impartation of your knowledge in a manner that enables them to better understand that which you already know.

4.) Add perseverance to your self-control. Do not simply give up nor write things off as being impossible or unchangeable. The temptation to throw your hands up and cease the entire change process may be great at times. But press on. Anything worthwhile takes time. Remember, we are on a thousand-mile journey. Do not stop short.

5.) Add lawfulness to your perseverance. Shortcuts generally do not produce lasting results, and the ends do not generally justify the means. There is never a need to turn to violence to exact civil change. Dr. King was a model to us in this regard. Do not work around the law but rather work to change the law through allowable mechanisms. There are many nonviolent avenues for change.

6.) Add friendship to your lawfulness. Extend the olive branch of fellowship. Allocate to others the same latitude and grace you give to close friends and even family members. Spend time with them. Get to know them. Share life together.

7.) Add love to your friendship. Love has become such overused nomenclature that it often means anything or nothing. The inclusion of love in this list, however, is not the starting point but rather the endgame. Leading with love is antithetical to our human nature in matters of change dynamics. Love is not an emotion; it is a choice. It is choosing the best for another person, even to our own detriment. Such a choice can only be a reality after other steps have been engaged. It involves a commitment and a decision on our part to stand with others, sometimes at personal cost.

Recently, there was a noted professor from a prominent university caught on film screaming and cursing at a group antithetical to her ideology as they celebrated in some manner rather innocuously. She was, in that moment, the poster child for everything her students should not be . . . intolerant . . . unempathetic . . . and downright ill-mannered and mean-spirited. This is never the path for effective change. Her response, however, should cause us to ponder her own story? What journey is she on that would catalyze her to respond the way she did?

Are you able to extend an apology? Many people cannot. Apologies confess guilt, challenge our pride, and make us vulnerable. Given some of the actions throughout our national history, apologies are a necessity and often necessary multiple times. Such apologies cannot be hidden or subtle apologies but clear, open, and public apologies. Freedom comes when we open the closet doors and remove the skeletons completely. There is nothing easy or particularly pleasant about the process, but that cannot stop us from extending sincere apologies when they are clearly in order. They are the landmark moments of our thousand-mile journey.

Reconciliation remains the single most vital aspect of collective action. It is, however, achievable only if it is the stated and desired outcome of the majority populous. It is not achievable individually. While banging the reconciliation drum may seem onerous, it is the origin for true forgiveness and healing. It is that which can stave off the generational blight of hatred and bigotry while also creating cooperation and synergy. No federal program or institution will pierce the veil of these maladies—only reconciliation.

Granting pardons is an ancillary outcome of forgiveness and grace being married to practicality and pragmatism. Pardons that are not granted when they are clearly necessary and appropriate can leave segments of the population consigned to a species of enslavement, leaving the victim worse off than the offender. Pardon can be extended even if it is not requested, and it should be the role of all to extend this allowance with careful discretion, but otherwise quite freely.

Accountability will play a crucial role in any change process of this nature. Conceivably, this might be achieved through the development of entities committed to advancing the concept at a societal level. These entities must be innovative producers, a place for progressive thought, and subsequent evaluation of societal accountability at the institutional level.

Such a center of thought leadership would need to remain dedicated to gathering and synergizing sharp, unbiased minds—individuals committed to real outcomes and not aimless pontification and self-aggrandizing. Such a sodality would be fully committed to honestly understanding the full scope and nature of the clash of civilizations and power shifts occurring, both nationally and globally. Tracking demographic trends and their corresponding representation of those populations in the political, educational, business, arts, science, social, economic, and religious spheres of society would be paramount. The evaluative process would extend well beyond basic numerical representation into levels of true influential representation. Its goal would be to engage the broadest swathe of American society in advancing the change processes here expressed.

The United States of America rests on the precipice of an opportunity unlike any previously encountered. The nation is poised to demonstrate to the world that its strength and vitality will perpetuate itself, as evidenced by its peoples intrinsic ability to self-correct and adapt to a changing world.

The options are relatively simple. America can choose to celebrate and perpetuate the diversity of an evolving citizenry, or choose to isolate itself in fear. Will the nation embrace the collective contributions of its extremely diverse populace, or will it hold fast to archaic models destined for monumental failure? Refusing to acknowledge the inevitable power changes already underway will further complicate and exasperate the challenges lying ahead. Those challenges exist and will be confronted regardless of the nature of any collective decisions. The harbor is not a safe haven for the encroaching tsunami. We must leave the false security of the harbor and move out to meet the waves head-on and heart open.

These decisions transcend simply doing what is right or what is morally correct. They extend beyond acknowledging the beauty and value of other cultures, and certainly beyond dispelling the bizarre preoccupation some have with the dermatological facets of skin pigmentation and cranial phrenology. Now what is conceived here requires mutual trust and a commitment to justice, regardless of the price. It requires strength and courage as well as recognition of the scars we each carry and the fears that hold us captive.

The unseen forces working to separate each of us are not to be underestimated. Thomas Hobbs had it right. A favorable outcome, however remote it may now seem, is possible. It requires severe discipline and corporate self-control—a willingness to pause long enough not to formulate a defense but rather to fathom another's pain. Certainly, such a pendulum swing will not fully be achieved without forgiveness and many mutual tears.

If we are willing and prepared to traverse the journey together toward a mutually agreed-upon destination, then perhaps this road less traveled will lead us to the promised land Dr. King dreamed of. If it came to fruition . . . if it were truly realized, America would not only be stronger, greater, and more prosperous than we ever conceived but could conceivably break the invisible threshold on empire life cycles, as well as create a new standard for human civilization.

Diversity is one of the nation's greatest strengths and blessings. The first step requires an unwavering belief that America's true strength must be attributed as much to its diversity as it is to the original, unique, and marvelous construct under which it functions.

Epilogue

The Times, They Are A'Changin'

In undertaking the creation of this body of work, we, the authors, fully anticipated a wide range of critique and a spectrum of reactions. We welcome every bit of it, as neither of us believe we have even begun to fathom the depth nor the breadth of the subject matter herein addressed. Our goal was simply to introduce a thesis presenting inevitable power shifts, a framework for the current cultural environment, and to provide thoughtful and empirical validation of the stated thesis. Our goal has been and will be to ask each reader to begin to, or more deeply, consider how each of us should respond to these dynamics. We hope, if nothing else, that the truths we highlighted in these pages have become self-evident. If not, we are confident they will in ensuing months and years. May we be so wise, as is necessary, to minimize any negative impact and fully harness its positive potential in the days ahead.

Admittedly, we struggled with surmising the reading level we thought would prove most appropriate for the publication. At times, perhaps we erred on the side of not underestimating our readerships, but both of us agreed that we would speak to you intelligently. Our sincere hope is that your time spent reading this work proved enjoyable, yet stretching, and drives you to delve more deeply into the subject matter. Furthermore, we hope this work will appeal to as broad a constituency as possible and reach across monumental divides. We believe it will take a massive movement to respond appropriately to the changing tides and encroaching tsunamis, in order to avoid our historic pitfalls referenced in this book.

We are two white guys, and we acknowledge that may have been somewhat ironic in our effort to properly represent a variety of ethnic communities within the nation. Our backgrounds and vocational experiences have given us robust perspective, but certainly we have much to learn. We recognize the communities and affinity groups addressed are not homogenous, and that many ethnic communities were left unmentioned.

It may bring great satisfaction to certain readers to point out how weak our approach has been in terms of academic validation and rigor, including statistical support. We agree with that evaluation of our work but would argue that the vast majority of the academic evidence does fall in our favor and readily supports the thesis.

Instead, we approached this project in a manner that married a great deal of ethical and conceptual consideration, with a reasonable amount of undisputed empirical and statistical data. An appeal to the humanity, logic, and love of truth resident in most people was the framework in which we built our case.

Yet, what has been conveyed here covers such a broad range of subject matter that we inevitably risk offending certain students of the field in failing to recognize work that has come before us. Many excellent publications and treatises, wrought from high levels of expertise, have laid the foundation for the discussion at hand. Thus, we do not consider ourselves uniquely original. Unfortunately, those areas of expertise and subsequent writings are often disassociated from the mainstream, unnoticed for the most part.

Some dissidents may surmise we have a political axe to grind. Far from it. We have exercised extreme caution to avoid being partisan. Ironically, this approach is typically not lauded as partitioning common ground, so much as it is condemned by lynch mobs for the finite holes they can spot. Straying in any way from pundits' watchtowers is often akin to heresy. In a word, it is common to man to throw the baby out with the bathwater when approaching such deep societal issues. And while the authors recognize that the ensuing power shifts will have implications within the political forum, the impact on the broader band of the culture and, vicariously, the populous simply transcends this admittedly boisterous single sphere of society. These issues cut across the board, and the political chips may fall where they may, as the truth is laid plain.

As the title suggests, *Tsunami Watch* demands that we be vigilant but also decisive, taking initiative to avert and further prevent the undeniable byproducts of apathy and antipathy toward an inevitable shift in the national power structure. Power can be transferred in calm manner if structures are in place for the transition. The U.S. has much of that infrastructure in place; everyone needs to man their station and facilitate the process. A seamless process is a utopian concept, though, and power is seldom, if ever, transferred without some aspect of struggle and angst, whether violent or nonviolent. The tsunamis are inevitable but, with sufficient informed forewarning and decisive action, damage and devastation can be minimized.

We are not harbingers of doom but rather observers on a journey with our readers. We, ourselves, American citizens, proudly call this nation our own. We long for it to continue to perpetuate utility, peace, and joy for the hundreds of millions of its citizens. We want it to remain a beacon of freedom and hope, both for those who already call it home and for those who will one day make it their home. America's finest hours are before us, not behind us. But sustaining momentum requires honesty and sacrifice.

Sustaining greatness will be driven by the very principles upon which the United States of America was originally founded; the equality of all mankind, as well as the oneness of all mankind. Such a worldview holds firm that we are more complete, resilient, and indivisible because of our diversity and not despite it. May God continue to bless this Great Experiment.

ABOUT THE AUTHORS

Barry Christopher Howard

Barry Christopher Howard is currently the chief financial and administrative officer for New America, a think tank in Washington, DC, five hundred steps from the White House. One of his greatest joys is working with his colleagues at New America, to drive leveraged, measurable, and sustainable change in American society. For over twenty-five years, his career has been in the fiscal and operational nonprofit sector. Prior to his role at New America, Barry served as chief financial officer and senior vice president at World Relief, for over eight years.

Over the past two decades, Barry has served in varying capacities on the boards of several humanitarian organizations, international banking institutions (MFIs), as well as historic and civic nonprofit organizations. During his career, he has traveled to over sixty countries. Barry is an antiquarian book collector, genealogist and competitive chess player. He is interested in philosophy, theology, the classics, and the study of the American Revolution and its progressive impact on global society.

Barry holds an MBA from Johns Hopkins University and a BS in business administration from Regis University, where he graduated summa cum laude. He completed postgraduate studies at Harvard Business School. Barry and his wife, Amie, have four children and reside in northern Maryland.

Daniel D. Kosten

Daniel D. Kosten is the policy and advocacy assistant director for Skills and Workforce Development at the National Immigration Forum in Washington, DC. His role at the forum focuses on developing a constructive public conversation about, as well as strong advocacy for, the value of immigrants and immigration to our nation's labor force.

Prior to his work at the forum, Dan was senior vice president of US programs for World Relief, providing oversight for the organization's activities throughout the United States. Much of his program work focused on refugee resettlement, antitrafficking, and immigrant-related issues. Before his tenure at World Relief, Dan worked for nearly ten years in Africa—predominantly in the Democratic Republic of Congo and Cameroon. Dan initiated his international work in Africa as a member of the US Peace Corps and then worked with Christoffel Blindenmission, providing leadership for numerous projects internationally.

Dan was born in Taipei, Taiwan, and resided there until his freshman year of high school. He completed his graduate work at Wheaton College, with an MA in Missions and Intercultural Studies. His undergraduate work was completed at Calvin College, with a BA in political science. Dan and his wife, Holly, reside in Northwest Baltimore and have three daughters and a son-in-law.